MALE CIRCUMCISION AND INITIATION IN RURAL AFRICA

AUTOBIOGRAPHY, CULTURE AND TRADITIONS

Amadou Nouhou Diallo

AuthorHouse™
1663 Liberty Drive
Bloomington, IN 47403
www.authorhouse.com
Phone: 1-800-839-8640

First published by AuthorHouse   7/13/2009

ISBN: 978-1-4389-9632-5 (e)
ISBN: 978-1-4389-9633-2 (sc)

Printed in the United States of America
Bloomington, Indiana

This book is printed on acid-free paper.

This book is dedicated to my only son, Thierno Demba, and to my four daughters, Idiatou, Diaraye, Nylasia Safiatou, and M'Mahawa Nouhou.

MADINA BADIAR IS MY NATIVE VILLAGE, and it keeps intact its age-old customs and traditions. One is the circumcision or the ablation of the foreskin, done in a traditional way by the people of caste. This is a rite of passage marking the entrance to adulthood, setting the stage for that person's life. If he shows any fear, then he is a failure.

If one is deemed a failure, the resulting humiliation is so smarting, and the social consequences so important, that the shamed ones prefer to flee the village.

The ceremonies generally take place between the months of March and May. So an active group of five to ten men is chosen to be circumcised in a lapse of time defined by the customary chief and certain old sages. To practice the ritual, they take these young men far from the village.

The objective is to preserve the intimacy of the Beteebhe ," or the ones circumcised, but also, and especially, to keep the ceremony mysterious. This ritual is an educational function insofar as it promotes the survival, the knowledge of nature, the sexuality, the religious beliefs, and the social values of the community.

The "Beteebhe " that once lasted several months have been reduced to one month in order to adapt to the school calendar. Some socioeconomic changes have also deprived this ancient ritual of its spiritual and sacred dimension. A lot of adult men who are supposed to transmit the tradition leave their village for the city, in search of a better livelihood.

It's the men of the caste upon whom it is incumbent to preserve the tradition and responsibility of circumcision. It's them alone who have this legitimacy and this power.

At the time of the cut, the men must not blink. They must not show their fear; that would immediately disqualify them. Because the fear is judged to be proof that the "Bettie" didn't deserve to pass to adulthood.

In this case, even though the scene happened outside of the village, the news will have reached the ears of the local inhabitants quickly. The shame is great for the one who failed. And he is practically banished from the social life of the village. Among other things, he won't have the right to get married because one needs to be an adult to marry. The martyrdom is so intolerable that some escape to another region. The weight of the guilt is so heavy that some even go as far as killing themselves.

For those who were able with aptitude to achieve the ritual of passage to adulthood, the imposing ceremonies are spread over several days.

Aunt Binta had made the journey to take part in my circumcision ceremony at my village. I was delighted and even more delighted that she cared enough to make the long journey from her village, Woulandji Foutah, situated on the lower slopes of Mount Badiar.

At twilight, we arranged the instruments of the "Gunguey," which consisted merely of a large bowl of water covered by a calabash, which we hit with shorts sticks to ascertain the exactness of the sound. We also used a variety of musical instruments such as bells, musical bow, lute, and flute for melodies and rhythms. It had to sustain us until dawn.

Before going to the dance, we satisfied our hunger surrounded by our elders, who never stopped lavishing advice upon us while revealing the secrets of adult life so much that we already felt superior to our friends who were not ready for the circumcision, because of a lack of financial means or merely for domestic reasons.

When we were ready to go to the dance, my father asked to see me. Then he carried me into his round slot and asked me to take off my clothes. He washed me with a water of Talisman that he had prepared for me, then he made me sit near his bed while holding my bald head in his two smooth hands and whispered some verses of the Quran. "Go ahead, my son, don't be scared of anything. May God protect you!" he exclaimed.

In the end, we went to the dance. All our girlfriends were already there. Niang Mariam, my girlfriend, Tallatou, her sister, Habibatou my home girl, Fatoumata Titi, Kade, Yaye Bobo, Mama Assy, Aissatou, and so on.

This day my girlfriend approached me to show me love and compassion; she appeared to my eyes as the epitome of health; her skin was the color of a hemp grain, hot and shiny; her beaming forehead was vividly beautiful; her eyes were full of wonder and of sweetness. Faced with this audacity, our Baho judged necessary to tolerate our behavior. When she addressed me, her sweet heart and charm made me forget all my worries. Her voice was pure and clear. I felt that only truth could pass her lips and that all mischief and lies were banished. But, by over all, her eyes! The eyes expressed a confession: "To you, my love! I'm all to you in life, to you in the death!"

This day she was so beautiful that I remained mute, incapable of saying anything, standing before her, silent. I rubbed my eyes and looked away, then when I looked at her again, she appeared more beautiful, resplendent with the beauty of a girl loved by God, a girl chosen solely by Him, to show to the inhabitants of the Earth what can be perfection in a woman.

Then a real storm rose in my heart, upsetting all my emotions, a whirlwind that came to shake me thoroughly, raising like a dust cloud that came to darken my soul. Our Baho with his attentive eyes had understood the nature of the feelings that this girl had for me and summoned me to join the ranks.

We laughed and danced as we avoided looking like anxious candidates to challenge the test that waited for us. Our elders sometimes pampered us, sometimes intimidated us, such as when speaking to us about Manga Simbon, the one who had the delicate mission to proceed with our circumcision. They told us that this man had strength, magic to be among us without one being able to see him nor feel his presence. They even said that he could turn into a snake to inflict punishment on us if we appeared rebellious, just a way to prepare us for the resignation, I believe. They also told us that he heard everything that we said and saw everything that we were doing, being at home and six Miles from our village. There was indeed much to fear, but we took courage, although internally anxious and curious to see the veracity of what they just told us.

We continued the ritual dance as if nothing worried us. Also our cousins, sisters-in-law, and brothers-in-law teased us tirelessly in the paleness of the moon.

It was impossible to either sleep or doze. When dawn illuminated the horizon, I felt the fear wildly, but thanks to my determination, it vanished without being noticed by anyone. After all, I felt we had come too far, too close to the irreversible, crucial moment because people had changed their attitude of us and became less enthusiastic. Henceforth, people looked at us with mercy, knowing that the crucial moment was approaching. I saw my sister, invaded by fatigue, look at me as if to tell me to take flight, to escape this misfortune. Suddenly, our elders regrouped us and aligned us one behind the other and by order of family influence. The honor to be in the first place was given to me because my father was a big scholar (Master or "Karamoko"); he had the audience of an important number of disciples ("Talibes"). He made the translation and the commentary of the Quran, his daily occupation. The second place was given to Abdoulaye Telly, whose father was a respected and very popular man because he was the unique tailor of the village. The third place given to Yaya Labbo, whose father was the first muezzin of the mosque of the village, and so on.

After this very important ceremony, we surrendered to the River Diragodo, which ran by our village of Madina Badiar, to get us washed and purified. Under way, our Baho (who was the one who had to take care of us during the next thirty days) already began to give us some very rough orders.

We were intimidated but always determined to face the test. Each of us had two elders, one to the right, the other to the left. These people ordered us to walk with heads down and not to look to the left or to the right. They threatened us with wrong and shortcoming, so that I asked myself to my very depths how these people who were sympathetic with us all night long could change attitude so brutally? It was a real early and painful test that we underwent. We were so tired and so unfortunate that we didn't know anymore what holy to vow ourselves. In spite of it all, the resounding noises of the night, the laughter, the hugs with the girlfriends, the teasing of the cousins, and especially the warbling songs of the old women were even vivacious. We walked, avoiding the common road leading to the river, because they told us to avoid the wizards of the village who might fiendishly set deadly traps for us.

At the head of the line, our Baho used his local cutting blade to cut a path for us as we proceeded to our destination. Soon we arrived at the proper place, where we had to receive practical lessons of body purification. We also learned some signs and codes so that during our adult lives we could use them if we needed to.

It all happened quickly so that one thing came after another. Although the Gunguey dance lasted all night long, this ceremony of purification took us only thirty minutes.

Therefore, we started the process of returning to the village the same way we had come. The fury of our Baho and the requirement of our elders were at their height. When we were around the village, we saw the round slots sprinkled between orange trees and elderly mango trees, which sporadically extricated an early smoke. We heard the roosters crow, the dogs bark. All of it constituted the brightness of Madina Badiar, our village.

Our Baho directed us to the scene of the ceremony. Here they welcomed us as heroes. The Griots, commonly called the "Gawlos" in Fulani language, sang our praises, and our families distributed money to them. In a word, each of our families appeared richer and more generous toward them so that while crossing the crowd, I heard one of them say to cherish me while mentioning the history of my family, from my grandparents to me. I heard him speak of Thierno Malick Diallo, my paternal grandfather, who was a famous, well-educated, and respected religious man, and of Fode Kaba Doumbouya, my father's maternal grandfather, who was a warrior chief who fought against colonial domination in West Africa. It was indeed glorious, and the brightness of the moment was immeasurable. We entered a round slot not far from the crowd where copious meals awaited us, copious because my stepmother, who represented my deceased mother, had slaughtered the biggest cow of our herd for this special event. Not to mention that each of my mates' families had granted the same efforts.

They had us take seats on a very special rug, newly made of raffia, while our elders argued about which dishes to offer us. Finally the unanimity was reached and they gave us the dish prepared by my family, and the rest of the dishes were given to our elders.

I was filled with moral satisfaction; without this, one cannot alter the concern that I concealed mischievously because I felt that it was inevitable due to the hard test that we were going to undergo from one moment to another.

This time we ate without appetite; they even forced us to finish our common dish, part of the policy so that at the end of the thirty days we would come out strong. But our worries were hardly concealable.

After the meal, we went outside and the crowd cheered us stronger. I heard the same praises pronounced to my attention by the Griots (the Gawlos); the women including our girlfriends cooled us with the help of their scarves while the drums, the balafons, and the violins grew stronger. They quickly aligned us according to the recommended order. My mates and I knew that this was the last stage before the test. Therefore, we started walking toward the mosque. It was a silent walk; not even our elders were agitated, and our Baho appeared neutralized this time because everything that had to happen didn't have anything to do with him. All the dignitaries of the village were seated in a circle under the octogenarian tree overhanging the mosque. Among them were the people who came from Sinthiourou Mody Abdoulaye Dougoun Tunny village, where my deceased mother originated, of Sareboido, of Marou, of Kamabi, of Paounka, of Sounkoutou, of Doulo Oury, of Koundara, and so on.

Within five minutes of our arrival, the whole crowd that we had left behind joined us in silence.

They said that in the history of our village, they never saw such a number of people assembled. For protocol reasons, they ordered us to wait behind the crowd. The "Alphadyon" was forbidden since the independence of our country in 1958, but he continues to exist moderately either by nostalgia or by love of size. Therefore, he took the floor to insure that all dignitaries of the village were present and that all the requirements are satisfied . He spoke slowly and calmly as if every word that he pronounced was the last, while often scraping itself his throat. All that he said was transmitted in a high voice by his speaker, although each could hear.

He began to thank everyone. He asked if all dignitaries of the village were present, and it was necessary to confirm or invalidate it. When this procedure was over, they called us one by one to take our place in the crowd in a circle formed by the dignitaries. Each of us sat before a Master of the Quran, sitting with their feet crossed comfortably and holding in their hands an enriched white dress and a slate made of wood covered with Arabesque writing. Immediately, my Master of Quran told me gently to sit down. He stretched the white dress toward me, then asked me to remove my clothes and carry the new white dress , then to remove my trousers. I did it without delay. I don't know by what miracle he noted that I still wore my underwear.

He smiled with his flowing beard and told me that the underpants must remain there as well. Immediately I rose to remove my underpants while returning him a short smile of obedience. I was done quickly so I sat down again to wait for my mates to finish.

During this time I looked left and right. I saw these old men continually caressing their white beards, scraping their throats, chewing their kolas with their toothless mouths; a long time, I told myself, all these people saw me being born and saw me grow up in this village. All these people wanted to make me a worthy and capable man. A capable man to defeat without being defeated.

All these reasons were more reasonable and encouraging to undergo the test. When my mates were ready, we began the reading of the Quran. I knew by heart all the verses on the slate; I wanted to recite them without looking at the slate but my Master of Quran refused. It was necessary that he read them for me and I repeat them for him. Once the reading of the Quran was finished, the old men, one after another, made a display of their knowledge of the Quran to bless us.

Alphadyon had the right to make the last speech. Once again he thanked everyone while insisting on the respect of the prayer and practice of forgiveness. Suddenly, he announced that the ceremony was over and then he put us in the hands of our Baho. With honor and joy, that one immediately ordered us to align according to the established order. Then we began a silent walk in direction of the place of circumcision a few miles to the east of the village, in a very mysterious forest. This day, on a morning that announced itself without clouds (although the season was the beginning of the winter), two cyclones blew furiously. They joined to become a hurricane. Our very light white dresses floated in an instant. But could it be that this hurricane didn't blow for nothing? Could it be that this was the union of two geniuses that took place?

In spite of it all we continued to walk, our minds full of worries but always determined to finish. Here we are at a place that seemed all plain, so that I asked myself if this was really the place described to us. I saw five stones aligned one after the other. As soon as our elders ensured that no indiscreet presence threatened the mystery, they aligned us each behind a stone. I told myself that this was what the five stones were here for.

Each of us had one elder behind him. They turned up our white dresses and covered our eyes with their hands to stop us from looking at what had to happen to us. I felt that the act was imminent and irreversible. I trembled from head to toe. My mind, though full of fright, was alert. Before each of us could understand, the games were already played. Manga Simbon, with an illuminated stroke, finished circumcising us, and five rifle volleys were fired one after the other to indicate to those remaining in the village that five of us were effectively circumcised.

Suddenly, I felt a strange pain as if my body parted with my soul. I especially took fear when I knew that no sanitary measure had been taken. No anesthesia, no alcohol, and the knife that served for the circumcision had not been sterilized. We were on our backs. I opened my eyes, satisfied to have passed the most awful test. When the twilight advanced and the intimidating face of the forest grew dark, mixed in the splendor of a sky illuminated by a sun that got lost to the horizon, our Baho decided that the moment was auspicious to join the village. We left the place with the biggest merry-go-round and moved in the direction of the village, where the members of our respective families waited for us.

They cried for us, and compassion was in their faces because of the pain that we suffered since the morning. That's when I felt the emptiness that my mother left around me. I understood that the mother is irreplaceable. A feeling of mercy won my soul, so that my eyes whimpered discreetly. People quickly understood my pain. No one wanted to cross my heavy look of fear to sadden me more. The tears overflowed. But they were in vain because my heart consumed itself. I lived through this day in the deepest of despair, difficult hours, but decisive of my orphan's life.

The Griots, always invading, exerted nothing to exacerbate my wild pain. They were only interested in my mates, whose mothers were all present. Singers, satirical fabulists, and some famous humorists were present, to the delight of the participants. I ended up therefore acquiescing to the circumstance and threw a mitigating look at these Griots, who did not want be quiet. When this short but very significant ceremony reached its end, people dispersed themselves and the night advanced. However, the bursts of laughter of our childhood girlfriends, our brothers, and our sisters sounded in the middle of the night and made me want to join them under the fattening pond of the moon.

But it was impossible for me to do so. I told myself then, in spite of it all, I remembered and would always remember the memories of my childhood in my native village, Madina Badiar, by the orange trees, the gigantic mango trees, the vegetation, the fauna, and the beauty of the natural landscape and the panorama of the Mount Badiar, which gives the village its name. It explains itself by the living content of the values of his forebears and the significant hospitality of its inhabitants. Even if it is obvious that the influence of the West is present everywhere in Africa, in my village it remains unnoticed. While my mates slept and even snored, my eyes were still open and staring at the roof. Every time that our Baho lit the lamp to insure that we were all right, he saw my open eyes and gave me the order to go to sleep.

Very early the morning, I received my father's visit. He came to ask me to be courageous because he had been seized by our Baho, who was worried about my very troubling attitude. He implored me to stop thinking about my mother. He told me that he wanted me to stop it and to count on him. This day, I saw for the first and last time tears in my father's eyes. A merciful grief invaded my soul, and I trembled in a delayed attitude. I held myself for quite a while.

"Listen, you must not have this poor old man mourn," I said to myself. When my father left, I made a sign of relief. Since then, I seized myself forever. On the following day, my Mother-in-law , came to apologize to me for having been absent at the ceremony of welcome and not offering me a gift like my mates received from their mothers. But yesterday I made the resolution to not collapse for any reason because my father had told me so. When she rose, not to hand me a gift but to take leave of me, I felt a lump rise in my throat. My eyes were so full of anger. I used my right hand to keep my mouth shut against a possible outburst. Fortunately, the lump that went up my throat even dimmed itself.

Suddenly, the force to defeat the sadness assured me a subtle peace. Nothing interested me anymore. Listen to me, young man, said our Baho, in all things it's necessary to remain calm. You became a named, full and whole man to ensure your own future. You must not move back from any obstacle. Nothing must frighten you or exceed you. Know that the father and the mother constitute the fundamental basis of a man's life. But this basis, even as essential as it is, is not the end of a man's life. Therefore, you are required to live your own life. Your mother is not alive anymore, and whatever you do, she will never come back to life. Therefore, stop moaning yourself.

It was necessary to wait for seven days before beginning to clean and medicate our wounds. We all knew that this phase, although final, was not an easy thing. A heavy odor began to invade us. Every evening around a wood fire, we learned the history of our village, its forebears, secrets, and perspectives. They told us so much of this village, so that we believed that the universe limited itself in the drill. During the thirty days that we remained under the ascendancy of the circumcision, we perpetuated the memory of our forebears. "Byllon," the blacksmith of the village, this human library with his universe of knowledge, had been charged with teaching us all the secrets that our forebears bequeathed us, which we were judged incapable of knowing before our circumcision.

A lot of youngsters had left our native village to continue their studies or to look for work, believing that life was better elsewhere. In spite of it all, each of them had been initiated into the secrets of the village before leaving. We trusted in the future of our village and in the future of this world in spite of the horrors and the difficulties which we confront.

Byllon, this verbally enterprising man, had many things to tell us. That night, our Baho summoned us with the order to stay silent. Then Byllon, with a smile, began his narration with a realistic and intelligent analysis of the way Western civilization has brought prejudice to our customs. He mentioned to us the things that don't exist anymore in the village, because the totalitarian regime demystified the secrets. It's why threaten disasters don't save our village anymore. The drought advanced because a lot of secrets were unveiled. He remembered that our village had astounding beauty. The green lush of the valleys combined with the emerald waters of the immense Mount Badiar. Its charming landscape by its beauty and its abundant vegetation gave us the impression of living in an earthly paradise.

But today it has all disappeared. This man was so eloquent and so intelligent that I understood that the African oral tradition was especially experimental. Whereas in the West, the theorizing of knowledge is systematic. All men, no matter their cultural background, construct a unique personality.

I also understood that the man had the noble mission to awaken our potentialities lulled by adolescence.

Can it be that as fearing all secrets of the village will probably happen to reconsider our fundamental archetypes in order to always have an attachments to our traditions.

Finally I realized that life in our village was in perpetual mutation.

Byllon was a simple enough man. A man of exception, always smiling and ready to hire his comedy by cultural time, by artistic time. He never tried to say that he was a ferryman and not a blacksmith. Between the two, he preferred the one that God gave him that wants to say ferryman; ferryman of knowledge of one generation to another. He seemed to be poet and local philosopher. He allied a vast culture, a superior intelligence, and an extraordinary charisma. I always remember his fine silhouette and his friendly smile.

A week later, very early in the morning, toward 5 a.m., we journeyed to the Journdhe River, to start the treatment process. I confess that this stage, although last, was the hardest. The process consisted of putting us naked under the river's water. It was over our heads by fifty meters.

The orders to separate the legs to expose the sex half were firm and without appeal. Our Baho and our elders had all made arrangements to endow themselves with a heap of whips with which they hit us without mercy.

None of us were prepared for the pain. The screams and the tears of my mates and myself brought up strident echoes in this sacred river, in spite of the noises of the frightening water waves of which they speak to us so much.

Soon we could see the crocodiles come out from their shelters to take a sunbath on the banks of the river. According to statements of the one and of the other, our Baho had strong magic to neutralize them. Once this test ended, another one lurked.

This was about pouring the excerpt of the salve of a tree called "Syndiah." The flesh of this tree is a real antibiotic that protects the wound against all infection. On the following day, we surrendered to the Journdhe River while taking the usual early chore. But we had slept badly. Byllon had certainly not been foreign to this insomnia. But an essential preoccupation had resulted from us, even awake. We dreaded the tests that we had to undergo, and besides, the anguishes of the nightmare gnawed us even stronger.

And then we felt, in our flanks, the trip of anguish that invaded our souls while thinking about this vast furious rock moistened with Talisman of all sorts on which we had to take place. He was unusually more extended and more spacious. But the caprices of the river made it less accessible, because to go there, first it was necessary to face the assault of the waves and a bunch of slippery and dreadfully pointed rocks.

This process consisted of washing our body on top of the diabolic rock. When my turn arrived, although this diabolic rock was desolate, while heading toward it, a masculine voice made me jump, and I believed I was in a strange world. I stood up hastily and took a decent position. A octogenarian man looked at me and laughed in a high voice. Not far from the snarling cascade of water, where the women washed linens, songs of love began. However, in normal time, this place is relatively restful and aside from all animation. Suddenly, our Baho told me, "Go, my boy; do not be afraid, these are the owners of the sacred place. They are naturally nice. You must continue to advance toward the rock, not to have to restart all over again."

All of a sudden, everything went blank and I sat on the rock facing a calabash filled with water. I wanted to take the calabash in whole to pour its contents on me and to leave this furious place if possible.

But this calabash, although small, was so heavy that it was impossible for me to raise it. During this time, our Baho, our elders, and my mates contemplated the scene with enthusiasm and laughed strongly. I was obligated to respect the whole procedure.

On the third day, Byllon presented himself earlier than usual . He always arrived with empty hands. Books and notebooks didn't make sense to him, not knowing how to read nor how to write. However, the oral tradition had made him a perfectly aware man. Therefore, the theme of the night was the "Waadju," that is, moralization. A good moralist, he spoke to us of customs, nature, and the human condition.

What impressed me was the methodology of Byllon, his dynamic and living character. Let's avoid the labeling to consider the adventure of his own self-knowledge. While listening to it, we could even learn to go to the bottom of us, to know us indeed. It has permitted us to become internally more harmonious as well as in our reports with others. I have been charmed to find, within my own culture, a philosophy close to the contemporary world. In a word, the rich and varied African culture is the one that frees man and awakens his sleepy potentialities.

While fearing it, we will manage, as Africans, to reconsider our fundamental archetypes while ensuring the transmission of generation to generation.

When Byllon approached the Waadju, a sort of psychotherapy, he supported firmly that an individual's process means how he developed himself, how he continued to lock itself in something that doesn't invite him in, and how he can react to get out of it no matter his culture. There, the euphony gesture is even more global. Not only does she integrate the emotional, intellectual, and spiritual physical reality of the human being but she goes farther. The methods that she puts in place allow the individual not to see itself like a cultural schema but to know itself directly by servation.

I look at myself to function and I note how I react. On the basis that it knows itself in order to rid himself of the influences that developed in itself of the aggression, of the revolt. Gradually, a man can free himself of his conditioning of what he acquired since childhood and he can integrate mechanically by time.

Taking advantage of a short pause, our Baho attracted the attention of Byllon on the fact that the theme was superior to our level of comprehension. "Don't forget that you are dealing with kids!" he exclaimed.

Byllon appeared unsettled by this remark, which he didn't expect. But very early, with a remarkable elegance, he chose to agree with the remark.

However, the impact of the surprise had already affected his enthusiasm, which began to fall away. In a loud voice, he declared that today's vigil was finished but the next day's would be more interesting.

This brutal measure saddened us because we were fascinated indeed by what this man told us. I understood personally, before everything, that our cultural heritage was again in the oral tradition. This is how the transmission of the knowledge, the religious teaching, the initiation to the myths, the education of the children was transferred from generation to generation. The oral literature was always and remained again the ideal shape of expression in a farming environment, where the majority of the population is illiterate and leads a communal life in the outdoors.

Life in my village was bound closely to the practice of raising beef, which we pushed before us, always in search of new grazing land. Installed on the high trays of Mount Badiar, we kept intact the nearly millennial traditions of our forebears.

The pastoral life of the Peulhs, which we are, included a set of magic practices that expressed itself through rituals, one life-style bound to their pastoral activities.

Their vision of the world, their conception of life, their passion for the raising of beef appeared through spoken pastoral so-called poems and acts. They believed deeply in the virtue of the words, of its force, and the efficiency of the speech, and they think to be able to master and to domesticate the occult strengths by symbols, rituals, and magic formulas.

In short, we won't ever finish describing the universe of this ethnic group deeply attached to its millennial tradition.

With the Peulhs, the oral tradition is not only narration of historical exploits for the reconstitution of the history of a locality or a population, it transmits all shapes of the culture.

Of all its shapes, the song is one used the most. Although the use of the song in the daily life varies according to history, the customs, and some specificities of the traditional society of Peulh, we can affirm that it constitutes, for her, a shape privileged of education, an efficient means of expression.

By the shape and its content, the song marries the contours of the society that created it. In traditional African societies, the songs in their shape, their content, or the rituals that surround them, vary from one region to another.

After the departure of Byllon, our Baho ordered us to sleep because tomorrow's departure would be very early.

At 5 o'clock in the morning, while we snored in concert, our Baho woke us up. Immediately we started walking toward the river. At midway, we stopped to extract the sap of Syndiah to treat our wounds after the bath.

The Syndiah is a tree endowed of medicinal virtues, and it grows perfectly in tropical climates. It contributes to the recovery of a certain number of illnesses in farming communities.

We arrived at the river to get under the waves of water, as this was the routine for several days, but this time the test was not so hard because our wounds had finally healed up. Our Baho was so relieved that he didn't stop teasing us as if we were now out of all danger. "Tomorrow, we are going to hunt," he exclaimed.

With serene enthusiasm, our Baho decided to delay our exit in order to put it more to profit. This is how we left the river to engulf us in the forest, characterized by the presence of a mountain chain like the belt dominated by Mount Badiar. This forest, whose flora is very rich and varied, is also covered by medicinal trees with all species. We identified some like the following:

1. Chimmeyhee. This tree has the medical virtue to heal tumors and gangrenous wounds. Some even affirm that if this tree is scientifically analyzed in depth, it could contribute to neutralize or even heal cancer or AIDS. Its leaves, its bark, its roots, and its sap are all medically useful.

2. Syndiah. This tree whose sap healed our wounds is a carrier of incontestable medical values. It contains natural and medically perfect antibiotics.

3. Telly. This is a tree whose bark produces a real poison, often used for offensive means.

We found different species, sometimes nourishing, sometimes medical, and sometimes harmful. We took the day to profit. At the end of our journey, we collected dry wood. Each of us kept a faggot to deposit with his family to help light the kitchen fire. Our very satisfied parents blessed us without reserve.

In fact, the role of traditional medicine concerning health care in the developing countries is well known and accepted. The importance of the contribution of natural products in orthodox medicines cannot be ignored. For the majority of the population that lives in farming zone in Africa, the traditional African medicine is the pillar of the primary health care.

Since he was created, man always counted on the resources of his environment to survive. The plants, the animals, and the minerals constitute the main natural resources used by man for the promotion, the prevention, the treatment, and the adaptation in the domain of health.

In Africa as in the other continents, these resources have been used over ten thousand years by the traditional practitioners who have acquired their knowledge and their ability to produce through observation, spiritual revelation, personal experience, and the formation and direct information of their predecessors.

In general, traditional African medicine is based on a global approach with regard to the patient's management, which carries on the body, the soul, and the mind. The recourse to traditional medicine is a universal reality in the sense that it has been used since the existence of humanity everywhere. In spite of the insufficiency of the proof of its efficiency, traditional medicine is used for the management of different illnesses, from the illnesses of spontaneous recovery, to those that can be deadly.

Indeed, in most cases, traditional medicine is, for these populations, the only available and affordable health care. In such a situation, the important condition of traditional medicine as the main provider of health services in Africa is always taken into account.

After twilight, and after dinner, our Baho informed us that very early the next morning, we would be at the disposal of Kotto Souley, who was the biggest hunter in the village, and otherwise the most famous in the region.

In this particularly hot and hostile tropical climate, our Baho required us to go with him to hunt to bring back to the village the meat of bush, the only way to demonstrate that we became indomitable warriors.

Kotto Souley had the face of a hard but just man. Usually he hunted the bush to sell meat to the villagers. At the end of every season, he always returned with the most skins of marketable animals. He was a gigantic and well-muscled man. He had learned the martial art during his adventure in the country of Terranga, which made him a dangerous man. He gave us orders here and there. He never addressed our Baho directly, since he overtly despised him.

Our Baho in return looked at him with a religious devotion that contained a good part of terror. We didn't debate his orders. We suffered for him, and if we came back to the village, we only bragged a little to have been hunting with him. He was an extraordinary, hard, and inaccessible man. Every year his prestige provided him with about ten circumcised teenagers, shivering with fear.

We always left at dawn with Kotto Souley at the head of the line, preceding us by some remarkable meters.

One day when we had just left the village, a panther screamed behind us. Clearly outraged, Kotto Souley gave us the order to go out, kill it, and bring back its skin.

Armed with many rifles, we headed toward the animal. The more we advanced, the more it became furious and unmanageable. Feeling threatened by our defiance, he made a frantic jump to disappear in the immense forest.

We believed ourselves threatened. In the fright and confusion, we took flight and returned empty-handed to Kotto Souley. Our friend, Yaya Labbo, had run into a tree trunk and was wounded. He had put his right foot into some burned tree stumps. We were obligated to stop and rescue him. When we came back carrying an injured hunter instead of the skin of the panther, Kotto Souley inflated his enormous chest and became more furious than ever. Suddenly, our Baho told him, "Kotto Souley, it's over; let's return to the village, because we have an injured hunter."

"You are crazy to return. Imbecile, don't you have anything in the brain? To lose one day of hunting for youngster's who was idiot enough to get himself wounded. What's wrong with you? Put him under this tree for me; we'll pick him up on our return."

At that, his anger changed itself into big fat laughter, and our Baho, although a bit heartsick, also started laughing, to not be left out. All was forgiven.

We walked for hours in the forest, and we finally met face to face with the same mad panther, recognized by his twisted left foot; in his merry-go-round, he believed he had avoided us for good. He didn't have a choice; he understood quickly that to run was no longer the solution. He decided to face us while screaming his defiance. But alas, Kotto Souley, in a lightning and courageous gesture, pulled the trigger of his rifle to send a bullet into the animal's head. The panther was dead. A white and boiling liquid came out of his mouth. Kotto Souley knew in advance that the skin of this animal must not be damaged to risk making it nonmarketable; he insisted on cutting it at the nape.

"Gentlemen, come help me. The strongest first," he said. "The bigger the panther, the more his pelt is worth. It's only in final season or when the hunt hardly smiles that we take the young panthers."

An experienced hunter, he skinned this animal, defeated by human cruelty, in three strokes of his large knife.

He turned it on its back, split the stomach with one stroke, then a stroke on the left, one on the right, and finally he pulled the skin, which came off easily. The bloody carcass was abandoned there, where it was immediately covered by a dark and loud influx of vultures. Toward the evening, drunken of blood, the birds, wings and heads stained, retired heavily toward the cliffs.

The skin of this animal was rolled carefully in the foliage of trees, freshly picked for this effect. We carried it one after the other. As promised, we paused to pick up our patient. We found him shivering with fear in this forest infested with lions, panthers, and snakes of all kinds. Immediately he asked us for water to drink but Kotto Souley interfered, saying, "My boy, stay; come, we don't have time to waste. You're going to drink to your manner once we arrive in the village."

Abdoulaye Telly and I carried him to the village, while the others continued to carry the panther skin.

Kotto Souley prayed, in a whisper, his face turned toward the Orient in an attitude of contemplation, to ask God and to solicit the intervention of the geniuses of the bush in order to protect us against all pain, but also to allow us to defeat without being defeated. On our return to the village, it was our turn to begin in a high voice the incantations of poems to indicate to the villagers that we had come back from a hunt that was fruitful. The curious people who wanted to know what kind of animal we had cut down came sporadically out of their round slots to contemplate us on the path. They looked at us with a lot of attention, and I felt big and invincible.

In the heat of the month of May were some small squalls of wind that pushed before them, as tops of the whirlwinds of dust and sand. It was in this little pacified tropical climate that men and women looked at us to pass.

Speechless, they watched Kotto Souley, a silhouette who was familiar to them, pass by. They shouted to the children not to embarrass the passage. But there were among the adults those who didn't inconvenience themselves and continued their occupations placidly while glancing.

Although they heard either the sarcastic voice of our Baho or the authoritative stamp of Kotto Souley, their indifference held until the end.

We continued walking to deposit our load at Kotto Souley's, who was the undisputed owner. Once we arrived, he invited us into his abode, eight meters by six, where light never penetrated a door or a window, and plunged in a semi-obscurity; a brown table, an amphora in clay, two small benches, two straw chairs, and in the bottom, against the wall in palisade, a shelf. However, we saw there an elegant detail, a coquetry: a bed made of iron, nearly new, from the country of Terranga, which exhibited itself in the least dark part, and on this bed, a work bench that could serve as a mattresses. We could not imagine a more Spartan setting, but Kotto Souley seemed satisfied.

Arriving at home, our Baho hastened to give the care necessary to our patient, which undoubtedly comforted us. However, he exerted to appreciate and exaggerate the skill of Kotto Souley to have brought the panther down. But we opposed it with a very remarkable indifference.

To analyze and to understand the physical misery in which we evolved, I was able then to affirm my inability to reach a conclusion without the least risk of straying between the traditional world and the modern world.

In spite of it all, I had an impenitent optimism that, in all analysis, I refused to believe the radical pitifulness of our contemporaries.

I kept myself carefully away from all controversial subjects that could be interpreted as a demonstration of tepidness to them. We were so tired and so quiet that our Baho ordered us to sleep very early.

Deeply asleep, I dreamed the advent of a new day, and I greeted with enthusiasm the forebears of my village, who surrounded me. This dream expressed the obsession of these forebears because in my village, a lot of mysteries were demystified. I woke myself up and stayed awake for quite a while.

Early in the morning, when we had just hardly awakened, the male nurse came from the Protestant church of Paounka, situated seven miles from my village, to examine and to treat our patient, because the customary rules that surrounded the circumcision didn't forbid it. This male nurse, far from being qualified, hardly knew how to read and to write, but he had the maximal pride to be called "doctor" by the ignorant villagers, who had no idea how he received this title. His presence in our village provoked an early crowd of the curious or the medically needy persons. In record time, our hut resembled a public hospital. Doctor Sana distributed medication without prescription. All sick people, no matter what their pains were, had the right to some tablets of aspirin, whose expiration date was unverifiable. He and his cortege of soliciting persons kept us all a half day. We felt comfortable that Doctor Sana enjoyed well in our village that is an animate and convivial place where the smile and the good mood are quite impressive . However, I recognized that in my village there is love for me that I didn't receive anywhere else. It is simply so fascinating. It is Madina Badiar of every day with its scenes of the current life. It is where I spent all my childhood. A childhood that touched me so much that it propels me right on my rack, and I feel it as the testimony of daily life with its blend of humor and mood.

I explored the marvels and the dazzling, countless treasures. All of it had made my childhood a decisive stage of my life. At the moment when Doctor Sana left us, Byllon arrived without notice. We were excited, knowing in advance that this man always had interesting things to tell us. He had the art and the manner to make us go to the seventh heaven as to break our hearts.

To transmit the oral tradition is indeed his domain, and he dove into it with a real pleasure.

His memory rolls itself up and takes place like an interior song, and it is the voice of the forebears that suddenly resounds, the one that imposes sharing, honor, and inheritances. Finally, the one who reinvents the traditional Africa.

Byllon doesn't land in doctrinaire of his own philosophy.

Well, on the contrary, he evokes the for and the against them, the toppling over that can occur between those who believe in pastoral traditional philosophy and those who don't believe. So all along his narration, at a time crackling and discerning, he mingles the various games of fantasy to secret preview on the deep reasons of the antagonisms that guide the world. Passion, hate, desire, racism, violence, and tradition. He is going as far as affirming with pertinence that the worse enemy of man is man himself. Because it is he who manufactures the weapons, fights the wars, tortures and kills his own species either because of jealousy, or for profit or for love of territory.

The animals only kill man to defend themselves.

Destiny only carries man by the will of the Lord. This supreme analysis only generates the truth; for simple purposes, here is a literary example.

Actually, Byllon is a blacksmith fascinated with the oral tradition. On the social plan, a blacksmith's role is the least that he is. He is not only the possessor of many secrets but his activities in the traditional African society are very productive. The blacksmith is from a caste where knowledge transmits itself from father to son. So one doesn't become blacksmith while practicing this activity but rather by birth. Therefore, it is not by a miracle that Byllon remains possessor of such a sum of oral knowledge. So one sings about courage and the importance of the blacksmiths. As in all epic songs of this kind, it is composed of comparisons, euphemisms, or symbols. It regenerates the young blacksmith and excites his courage and his sense of honor, which gives him the force to break the rocks, to cut the biggest trees, to make the dugout or the ax.

It makes an allusion to the feeling and to the thought of one precise time. Taking into account all these positive aspects, we can easily raise a conclusion that allows us to admit that the African tradition illustrates with strength the affirmation to be at the origin of the universal culture.

After one moment without a lull, Byllon noted our real satisfaction to see him among us. With his frozen look, I understood quickly that he tried to make us one revelation Immediately, he asked us to keep the silence.

"I don't come to maintain you but rather to see your patient," he said. One could read a certain disappointment from us, unrevealed but very obvious.

However, by the power of asking him many questions that deserved answers, he ended up changing his opinion. "I'm going to remain, therefore, to spend the evening with you," he acquiesced, before adding this: "You, the young of today, don't know your history, but when one speaks to you of it, that interests you. I felt in you a thirst for knowledge of your own history, and I'm delighted indeed."

We were filled indeed with joy and our relief was very remarkable.

First he answered all questions that were asked of him with the most clarity possible, then he insured that each of us was satisfied completely with the given answer.

The history of our village was, until then, little known. Those who had to deliver themselves to her reconstitution collected information piecemeal, more or less, from the notables. However, he said, "In my narration, I'm going to tell you one of the anecdotes that will allow you to live the atmosphere of the historic times bound to the existence of this village. However, it is necessary to mistrust the Griots in all their raving, which sometimes alters the facts. Know yourselves that an unforgettable and sad history has happened in our village. Over there to the southeast, nearly to the foot of the mountain, where this village was when it was populated, lived a noble, well-respected family. They had two twins, Alhassane and Alseny, well-fed giants, and black as coal.

"These two boys were so beautiful and shiny of health that all the habitants of our region spoke of it. One day in a dry season when the villagers had organized a hunt in the forest, to catch a doe and other various animals, the slave traders fell upon them, creating a total panic in the ranks of the unfortunate villagers.

"Some among them succeeded in escaping from these criminals, but Alhassane was captured with so many others. The slave traders were so impressed by the shiny beauty of Alhassane that they suspected that in the family of this young man, others may exist like him.

"They unbound him and appeared astonishingly very friendly toward him. Then they asked him if he had brothers and sisters. He answered ingeniously that he only had a twin brother. While his mates of misfortune were savagely tied up, Alhassane spent the night unbound but under heavy surveillance. Early in the morning, these criminal executioners, intoxicated with joy, made him promise: 'Listen, Negro, between your twin brother and you, it's necessary that one of you comes with us. Let's go therefore to the village to see if your brother will accept coming with us so that you remain free in the village.'

"Without understanding, he agreed himself to this false and smarting promise. First the chief of the executioners, knowing well the African tradition after practicing this profession of shame for many years, sent a mission to the chief of the village to ask him for the authorization to enter for merely friendly reasons.

"When the two missionaries of this black race arrived at the chief of the village, it turned into a meeting about the crisis that happened in the forest that they had precipitated.

"Around Thierno Yaya, the clear-sighted, indomitable chief strategist, and big Khalif, his son, who was called Mo-cellou Lekhol, who knew how to speak French and was barely literate before turning himself into big second-in-command of the village, there were also the big notables such as Mody Amadou Sare Guidho, Mody Mamadou Kossarey, Thierno Mamadou Alpha, Lassidan Mamadou Dian, Thierno Oussou Koin, Thierno Mamadou Dian Linguerey.

"All these big-headed, anti-slave traders were present. These two missionaries were marked very quickly and escorted before the chief of the village. When these two presented to the chief's court, they were bewitched by the place and by the very power of her occupants. Before delivering their message, they staggered for some seconds. When they finally transmitted it orally to the chief, this one perspired with anger. He wanted to strangle them to death. They tried in vain to calm him but his heart overflowed with rage. Suddenly, he exploded to laugh to subside his anger, then addressed these two strong men in these terms: "Traitors, kidnappers, who brings you to my village?"

But very early, the notables who surrounded him understood the stakes and tried to master their respected and very beloved chief.

"Okay," he said, "the white men can enter but only to this condition: first free our children."

The two messengers returned with their very heavy message full of consequences.

When they delivered it to their chief, this one did not take it in to consideration as it supposed to be .. Alhassane was bound again and thrown among his unfortunate fellow citizens.

By dawn, believing they were able to deceive the intelligence of the chief of the village and his brave citizens, these slave traders clandestinely entered the village and sped along directly to Alhassane's family, thanks to the help of this one who believed firmly to be able to rid himself from his executioners once they arrived in the village.

These slave traders didn't know that all big warriors and all big hunters of the surrounding villages had been scattered to the level of all strategic points and so they were ready to the assault. When they arrived at the family of Alhassane, at the order of his executioners, he called his twin brother in a high-pitched voice; Alseny hastened to answer, not knowing the danger that waited for him.

He rushed outside, having recognized his twin's voice, who he believed was finally free. But alas he met face-to-face with these slave traders with their cortege of misfortune. Alhassane, his twin brother, his hands bound behind, was hardly recognizable.

Tired, starved, and bruised by fear and the physical constraints, Alhassane told his brother, "The white man says that one among us must leave with them and the other must remain here in the village.

Do you want leave with them so that I remain or must I remain so that you leave with them?"

The white man and his interpreter exploded in laughter. But there is always you who wanted to stay! Suddenly, the white man pretended to be angry and said, "You will all come with us."

Alseny's hands were bound behind him. His parents cried out in a high voice, and the whole village was alerted. Then the villagers invaded the place, and the slave traders overflowed and began to pull the stocks of rifles, and the warriors and the hunters understood that it was time to make the assault. Very quickly, they advanced toward the enemy, now trying to flee with their captives. The partners pulled to the bright moonlight, as well as in the camps of the villagers, than In one of the white slave trader's camps, fought without reserve.

The villagers advanced and from elevation to elevation, their screams fed the ardor of the warriors, and the fury of the hunters spread panic in the adversary's camps. The chief of the slave traders, who understood that all was lost, took his rifle and planned to take the twins down; his heart was gripped in fear; however, he was still alert.

So diverting his head of a frightening jump, he took flight and his unfortunate partners followed him. The runners let themselves drive now by the fright, attentive only to avoid, while it was again possible that the villagers caught them.

Thierno Yaya, the head of his army, decided to pursue the enemies and possibly to free those who were again in detention somewhere in the forest. But seeing his personality and what he embodied, the villagers prostrated before him to ask that he grant them his blessing and his kindliness in order to allow them to fight the enemies in his name without disturbing his rest and his quietude.

The Griots sang its praises nonstop. But as a good religious man, his character hurt him and supported the promiscuity of these idolaters and their profane fun.

Finally he agreed to the grievances of those who that liked and admired him without reserve, and chose among them a man to assure the command. This choice was carried in the person of Samba Dannah. This man was constantly a rigorous strong man, ready to hunt or in quest of adventures.

As soon as he was chosen, all warriors gathered around him, the heads exalting themselves, the war against the slave traders of which, for a long time, already was in secret question, was decided firmly.

Being armed on the fields, the warriors pursued the slave traders to free their brothers, to avenge their deaths, and to triumph for their sovereign.

Coming out of Madina Badiar, they counted themselves; they were in all 299. Among them were again all the big, famous, and dreaded hunters. Full of a new courage, they hurried on toward their enemies, who eventually saw them coming and stopped to make a stand.

Immediately, Samba Dannah ordered the assault and pulled the bow string on the first arrow, killing a slave trader.

The battle became a free-for-all and fate appeared unfavorable to the slave traders. Saadu Hulata, who had a rifle (which few knew he had), began shooting; it struck terror into the enemy, and some believed that God himself came to the help of the villagers, slackened their defense, and fled in panic. The prisoners had been transferred to a secret place or even routed toward Ngore, the port of embarkation, since the beginning of the hostilities. Proud of their first success, the warriors, whose number increased enormously, because all established hunters had joined them here and there, pursued their enemies and in multiple engagements, inflicted on them new defeats.

Samba Dannah and his army came to camp, then to the foot of Mount Badiar in order to wage battle against a great deal of established slave traders in the region. The most successful were always increasing their enemies. By their courage, and their fearlessness, they were going to find a less radical tribal chief who, internally resolute, was to offer them a trap, pretending to assure them of all his friendship.

The army of Thierno Yaya advanced dangerously toward them. Its chief, Samba Dannah, like a toughened killer, was trying to wipe them all out, to sabotage their enterprise. They asked him to help to assure them victory over their enemies.

Pretending to be their genuine partner, he asked them to be fully reassured that he would do everything in his power to assure them victory as much by the strength of his fetishes as the strength of his influence. "Regroup yourselves therefore in my territory and to a hidden place to avoid the indiscretions," he said. "If God is willing, even though they advance toward you, it will be without danger because they won't be able to do anything except that to lower their arms." Then he sent them back without being given itself at the scene of useful information where they intended to retire.

Confiding in this promise, the slave traders left while the chief of tribes surrendered by Thierno Yaya. "I come to ask you for the command of the war," he said to him. "The enemies will be mobilized to Bouloubah in my territory, and we can now defeat them with God's help."

"It will be difficult," answered Thierno Yaya, "because they must be ready to defend themselves and they are well armed."

"Don't fear anything, Sovereign," said the chief of tribes. "I deceived them; they don't wait for us and didn't take any measure to defend themselves."

Then he told all measures that he had taken to know the exact places of their retirement and the defenses that they had arranged.

And his demand having been granted by his Sovereign, Thierno Yaya, with the help of Samba Dannah and his warriors, defeated in Bouloubah the enemies who had taken refuge in confidence.

This last defeat finished to terrify the slave traders of our region, who abandoned in mass their criminal enterprise in the whole Badiar.

When Byllon finished his history, we felt hypnotized and thrown into the clouds, so that it penetrated into our souls.

Slavery was a practice that lived its day in times past. It was deemed more profitable at the time, instead of killing and eating prisoners of war, to make them work. This practice existed with the Pharaohs of Egypt and also in Mesopotamia.

It was even blessed by Aristotle, by St. Paul, by St. Augustine, and legalized. It was thus a legal institution in Europe until the end of the fifteenth century. The antique bequeathed us of the free men ex-slaves, as Zenon, founder of the Stoa and the fabulist Aesop, to mention two of them only.

The Aztecs of Central and South America were the children of slaves, but had been born free while Europe in its American colonies "the raising of slaves while selecting some individuals in functions of physical criteria and while forcing them to have sexual intercourse in order to give birth together."

Some English and American capitalists had discovered that enormous profits could be accumulated thanks to the slave trade. And under the ascendancy of this stimulant, they made transporting the Africans to the New World, the most lucrative branch of the navigation trade. The best families, the nobles, the bishops, the princes of the commerce as well as politicians invested there heavily, and the English government took care of the defense of their interests.

"The poor wretches, pulled out of Africa by violence, were heaped as livestock in the fetid holds of the slave ships, places of darkness, foul air, and disease. If one lacked water or one was threatened with famine, or a pestilential illness occurred, the whole cargos of dead or of living slaves were thrown over the side by pitiless masters. If an isolated victim, tortured to lose reason, dared to raise a finger against his executioner, he was sure to be punished by mutilations challenging all description.

"The masters searched for the big athletic Negroes to mate them with the strong healthy Negresses. After having installed them in a room to part of the barracon, one obliged them to love each other, and the Negroes had to deliver a beautiful babies every year. They treated them like animals."

According to my own report, the most criminal damage was the fact that these slaves lost their identity, otherwise these people could have renewed today with their African origins. This statement of fact is a hard stroke for Africa but also a real psychological trauma for the black people on both sides of the Atlantic.

In July 2007, I had a cultural debate with a few African-American students from New York University. These students, hungry to know about their ancestry, asked me questions in a sporadic way. They wanted to know how to renew with their African origins. I briefly gave them the history of slavery, which they already mastered, and I specified to them that the difference between the African Americans and the Africans of Africa was solely cultural. We have the same fundamental origins and the same ancestors.

The world must not minimize or forget the suffering that the men and the women of Africa endured as the effects of slavery and its racist corollary. Those that triggered pro-slavery raids to the heart of Africa provoked tribal wars while exciting and arming the natives, knowing that these wars would bring them back their share of prisoners to fill their slave ships, indisputably committed crimes against humanity. If people of African origin do not have the right, according to some, to ask and to get reparations of the aftermaths, of the abuses, of the rapes of their body as their conscience, it's because the selfishness, ethnocentrism, and unhealthy and retrograde divisionism that continues to be enlivened by the big powers of this world with unjustifiable wars. The history of this tragedy has been overlooked, and it challenges black people to a deep awareness in view of a reinforced solidarity to break the gates trained against their economic and social progress.

It's why the Africans and the African descendants must share a common historic and cultural inheritance.

Many whites alter the historic belonging of the black peoples and ridicule their cultural identity.

In my humble opinion, I think that blacks, wherever they are, must work to give back life to the presentation of history and to promote the pride of their African identity while celebrating the diversity of their peoples.

In short, Byllon didn't want to draw a conclusion because the night advanced. We had to rise very early to consume our mush then to return to the summit of the mountain.

We fell asleep, our heads filled with new discoveries. We woke up very early in the morning, because we had not slept sufficiently. But it was a fundamental exigency because it was the day and the hour foreseen so that we began to eat lunch with the Labbou-Thièbhé, a sort of mush prepared with an extracted water scraped from the medicinal trees.

Consuming this mush would make us sexually very active even to the age of seventy. It is why it is not rare to see some old people in Africa giving birth even to the age of eighty. During the two weeks that remained, this would therefore be our daily lunch. This mush was bitter and difficult to consume; in order to finish the common dish, our Baho always beat us up with his big belt sewn of amulets.

After this early test, we walked toward the mountain with a considerable number of our elders; sometimes they appeared kind, sometimes mean. To reach the summit of the mountain, it was necessary for us to cross a vast tropical prairie poor in trees but very rich in animal varieties. The high herbs of the savanna, sometimes unmanageable, gave us a hard time. All the same, we could take a more or less direct path. The squawking of the birds disturbed us, but we didn't judge it useful to complain.

Suddenly, we arrived in a sacred place where it was necessary to implore the memory of our ancestors. This place was called Lombol River and was known to all girls and all boys of Madina Badiar because it was the place where you can ask and get the blessing of God and our ancestors. Each of us prayed and gave sacrifices. Others poured water and others deposited walnut kolas.

As a last resort, our Baho knelt before the consecrated rock to pronounce words in a low voice. We were indeed curious to know what he had to say but the mystery of the place kept us from asking. We were satisfied indeed to discover these places that we didn't have the right to penetrate before the circumcision.

Without having the time to admire them, our Baho ordered us to follow him, and our elders jostled us as if we had lost all our civic rights. We climbed on a big mass of rocks. It was a very difficult task. .

Finally, we arrived to the summit of the mountain and were surprised to find that there was a really big cow surrounded by a group of adults who were very recognizable. There were Kotto Bokar Niang, Kotto Baillo, Kotto Souley, Kotto Yaya, Kawu Abdoul Salamy, Kawu Amirou, Kotto Boubacar Barry, Kotto Thierno Souleymane, Kotto Ousmane Niang, Kotto Mamadou Mouctar, Kotto Telly Niang, Byllon, and many others. The presence of all these people astonished us, but the one cow in this very elevated place, nearly inaccessible, astonished us more.

Suddenly, calmness reigned before the elders insure themselves the right to give speeches. Finally, Kawu Amirou had the honor to take the floor. He traced the big lines of this ritual ceremony that consisted largely in teaching us how to master ourselves and the firmness every time it is necessary. We are going to slaughter and to cook this big cow, but the Beteebhé (or circumcised) would not taste any. But they will do the whole work for us, he said. The cow was brought down and slaughtered. The blood was recovered in a new calabash, which was placed under a diabolic rock venerated for several centuries.

While depositing the calabash of blood, Kawu Amirou, in an attitude of worship, tilted with extreme respect and implored the power that surrounds the mystery. He said this: "Oh you! Dhoddè Djinnah, or Place of the Angels, once again we come to offer you a gift of which you deserve well. You that never stopped watching over the children of Madina Badiar. It's you, morning and evening, under the hot sun and under the torrential rain, that protects us against the evil. We respect you and greet you all." He turned his head toward the crowd and asked, "Did I speak well?"

The whole crowd answered in concert, "Yes, you spoke well!"

As soon as he finished his supplication, Kally Gnywa, with his pastoral flute, began warbling a song of Peulh, and that engaged a mad ambiance that was completely controllable. These sacred places had an extraordinary, panoramic view. We contemplated from all angles a vast tropical landscape with its fauna and its flora. From there, we had a splendid view of our village with its mango and orange trees. Suddenly, we got to work, and they made us make everything there was to make because we were called one day to take the relief.

For many hours, we were busy skinning the cow under the attentive eye of our elder, who indicated to us the method to follow and the parts that must come back to the chief and the dean of the village, every time a cow was slaughtered in plain time in our village.

Very quickly we lit the fire, and the three big pots were used to cook a good part of the meat while the other part was burned to the fire of wood. Our elder digested this good meat, and our hunger became more and more acute. We were there the mouths flourishing of appetite. But alas it was positively prohibited for us to taste some even by curiosity. Once this feast ended, they submitted a hard test to us. It was about crossing a lianas bridge especially to test our bravery. This bridge raised over to the mountain frightened us. When it was my turn to cross the bridge, I got light-headed and lost my nerve. When I watched farther, I saw from the summit of the mountain of waters to flow furiously to the bottom of the valleys and others to throw themselves in streams. I barely got over my fear; my feet still trembled. How long would this cursed test last? When I finally arrived to the tip, I told myself, "Hey! There was more fear than danger."

By the time the ritual ceremony ended, the sun had already taken half of its journey. The trees swung their foliage to the will of the wind, which blew very strong. This time, to avoid the wizards, we used a different road that crossed a vast plain that spread as far as visible, and sprinkled here and there were golden islets, which were the fields of precious rice that was beginning to ripen.

During our walk, we met with an harvester of palm wine, who exaggeratedly sang in a high voice and without stop. For him nothing existed besides him. Every day from dawn, he penetrated nature only to return to his village at dusk.

The road always ran under this arch formed of bamboos and interlocking lianas. But sometimes the palms yielded the place to real trees to the rigorous and scaly trunks, encircled by lianas with an impressive green crown sustained by powerful branches. Of the trees solidly implanted in craggy soil, one spread madly toward a misty sky. It was troubling coming down on a twisting and narrow road through dark foliage sprinkled with scarlet flowers. It took us all day.

Thinking about what happened, I succeeded in making a personal report that brought me to affirm that the secrets societies had an occult and considerable role in the life of African people. They were even in the center of the resistance against the slave trade. Everything that we accomplished that day could have been a subject to be taught in class. But people of black Africa hadn't known from early on of the use of writing, and for a long time, this practice was reserved to a literate intellectual elite in Arabia. Again, it is why all our cultural heritage is in the oral tradition but alas, today it is neglected and may even disappear.

The African intellectuals have the moral and intellectual duty to prevent the wreck of our culture while adapting it to the new world. Our guilty indifference and the influences that come of all part murder our culture and place Africa in a retrograde position.

Our literature revives, illustrates, and defends the traditions and the great African values. Today part of this inheritance is put back in reason by a new generation of African writers who lean toward it by a so-called modernism. How ever, to remove or to overlook the African originality, that it is a country, a landscape, a typical character or a myth, would mean to fail to touch a part of the readership, interested by the diversity of the literature and civilizations.

In short, since we started on the path back to the village, Kally Gnywa continued in a high voice his incantation of the poems composed in free verse, expressing some invocation to the memory of our ancestors so that from afar, people admired us. It was already dark when we arrived at the village.

That evening, the moon surrounded by some stars went up gracefully on a firmament lounge of long white clouds and spread moonlight on the whole village. It was at this splendid moment that we arrived at our village, groggy from hunger but internally satisfied to have cleared a new stage.

We had hardly arrived at our hut, when big dishes of rice and meat were served to us, and we bounded on them as vultures with their prey. We ate our fill and quenched our thirst with water perfumed with the root of Guwe , which made the water even more refreshing. Then we yielded to a physical and mental fatigue that put us in a deep sleep.

Very early the next morning, the village woke up under thick, black smoke from an old car that evidently had stalled near our hut. This old 1940 French Citroen had been held together only by the finicky self-help of the rare mechanics of the region. It finally came to a stop before the hut that my father occupied. It was Mr. David Douglas who had come to greet my father and to bring him a contribution on the occasion of my circumcision. Mr. David Douglas was an African American who destiny brought back to the land of his ancestors. He had made my father his adoptive father, and he in his turn took him like his own son. He showed him all good paths to follow, and he defended and protected him everywhere. Mr. David Douglas came to Africa with empty hands but full of determination.

It was a true adventure but also a very moving resourcefulness in the eyes of each of us. He went from village to village, and people admired him like an angel and observed that between them and him, there was not any physical difference. It's rather the mental difference that was palpable but that, by the strength of things, shaded away gradually. They offered him some gifts in cash and in supplies that he kept intelligently .

Within one year, he got involved in agriculture, and some years later, he became the biggest producer of rice in the region. He bought agricultural machines and hired hundreds of villagers, to whom he paid a moderate sum of money.

He brought his wife Deborah and his son, Michael. This man who came from the southern United States had a very precise idea about agricultural activities. His nephew, Jerry, a construction worker, decided to join him. Thus, in addition to his agricultural activities, he also got involved in construction and saw himself immediately assigned contracts by the government. Other than French, Mr.David Douglas spoke three other national languages of the country. When his wife, Deborah, died due to a road accident during her vacation in the United States, he got remarried to Mariama Dalanda, a girl of a big royal family of the Fouta Djallon which, in spite of the barring of the Revolutionary Regime, continued to receive great respect on behalf of its disciples. His children are now a doctor, a professor, and businessmen. Everybody called him "Mister" and certainly didn't even know the meaning.

In short, Mr. David Douglas came to visit us and offered a beautiful bracelet watch to our Baho as a gift of encouragement. That day was the weekly market in Sareboido, and we asked our Baho to lend us the watch so we could go to make a "Tontah" with it, to make some money. This practice is only reserved for the Beteebhé, no one else.

The day being half consumed, he agreed. Therefore, he gave the watch to one of our eldest, in the name of Samba Sidibe, who called the other eldest to join us.

We went to the river, close to the bridge. All people who came back from the weekly market were going to pass there either to join our village or to go to the surrounding villages. Therefore, we deposited the watch in the middle of the road as if it was lost. Samba Sidibe, a very strong man, positioned himself behind a big tree just to look at the watch without being seen. The rest of us were regrouped a little farther away. This is how a first passerby saw this beautiful shiny watch lying on the ground. He stopped and looked at it without touching it. He started thinking but his sixth sense told him not to touch it; it could be a "Tontah" because there was a "Beteebhe" in the village. Or this watch could be a furious gift placed by the wizards or by the devils. He shook his big head and left without touching the watch, but turned around regularly to observe it before continuing on his way. We were therefore not able to do anything against him because the tradition says that it's only when the person touches the Tontah that he's liable to punishment of five francs..

Several minutes went by before a man who had just crossed the bridge while dragging his bicycle, because of the slope, saw this watch on the ground. Without thinking, he put it in his pocket and tried to hurry away before the owner came back to look for it. It's at just this moment that Samba Sidibe, from his hiding place, shouted loudly, "Tontah! Tontah!"

We all moved toward the fellow, our elder in front. Knowing the law of the Tontah and its misdemeanors, he didn't delay in paying us five francs before adding willingly some walnuts of walnut kolas, African symbols of respect and dignity. He was a man who lived relatively well because of his trade. He begged us strongly to keep silent because he didn't want the people of the village to learn that he took the Tontah, and we promised him firmly that the incident would stay buried from that minute.

He left then, his head low, his dignity wounded. Then we replaced the watch in the same place and went back to our hiding place to wait for the next victim. A half hour went by without another victim because others, by luck, passed without seeing the watch. It was then that a group of well-dressed girls, very fragrant on the occasion of the weekly market, arrived by the bridge, where they took enough time to quench their thirst and to chat. Out on the bridge, the watch was on the ground. Two girls hurried together to collect it but one only succeeded. The two argued furiously.

"No, it was I who first saw the watch."

"No, it's not true, it was I."

The one who collected it was a younger but bigger girl.

But the older girl protested loudly that the watch was hers because it was she who saw it first. In between, Samba Sidibe came out of his hiding place while shouting, "Tontah! Tontah!"

With an exaggerated gesture, the one who collected the watch hurried to give it to her friend, and this one in turn quickly moved far away from the watch. We surrounded them and required our due to the girl that collected the watch , who executed herself without delay.

The sun fell below the horizon and the night announced itself discreetly in this forest that pulls along the Badiar Mountain to the lower of which the opulent plains of rice culture sharpened the appetites.

Samba Sidibe and our eldest agreed that we needed a last attempt, and therefore we went back to our hiding place to wait. It was then that a man of about forty, walking as if he was asleep, collected the watch and kneeled to thank God for this providential gift, but Samba Sidibe didn't give him enough time to show his surprise. He left his hiding place while vigorously shouting, "Tontah! Tontah!"

The man deposited the watch where he was and tried to flee, but Samba Sidibe stood before him like a Sphinx. The man said, "I didn't touch anything, and you cannot stop me from leaving."

Then Samba Sidibe said to him, "will you pay or won't you?"

The man, answered "No Sir, I will not pay."

Then Samba Sidibe asked our elder, who arrived while running, to bring him a big whip. The man understood that it was more serious than he believed it. He said, "Okay, I touched the Tontah, but I don't have any money to give you."

Samba Sidibe told him, "Don't worry about it, you will definitely have something to give us."

When they brought the whip to Samba Sidibe, he told the man, "This is how you're going to pay us. We are going to hit you fifteen fillips, five for the Tontah and ten to have lied."

Choked with emotion, the man said, "No! Wait, I must have something."

He then turned up his traditional garment from the inside of his belt, produced a ten franc piece, and said, "Hold on to this, you can keep it all."

But Samba Sidibe told him, "We don't need it all but our due."

"Make the change then," the man answered, but it was impossible.

"Then you lie down; we are going to whip you," said Samba Sidibe.

"No! No! Wait, I remember." From the lining of his cap made of wool, he took a five franc piece and put it in the hand of Samba Sidibe, who thanked him with irony.

It was then our last ambush. We left the place to the twilight. The buzz of the birds in quest of sleep shelters constantly intensified. Wind and the dust screamed and collapsed in passionate waves on the trees gnawing at them. Also the growl of thunder, accompanied by the lightning that announced the beginning of the rainy season, had returned; the wind was so strong that it was necessary for us to raise our voices to make ourselves heard. That limited the conversation considerably.

From time to time, an even more vicious gust than the last raised our dresses and let them fall again like a child's toy. We now hurried as if we were pursued by danger, because we dreaded getting wet; that would foretell a bad augur on our future, according to the custom. Very fortunately, we returned to the village without getting wet.

Some hours later, this torrential wind with all its energy died on the horizon. Samba Sidibe returned the watch intact to the owner and stayed quiet.

"Let's go, Samba," said one of our elders, "tell what happened over there; you are dying to tell us, I am sure."

Samba smiled and turned toward our Baho and began to relate the story.

In the meantime, Byllon arrived with Mr. David Douglas. He had been invited by our Baho, who wanted to recognize him for his precious gift and help him learn our customs.

Mr. David Douglas had a strong intelligence but didn't know anything of the African tradition and only had a basic idea of what circumcision meant in rural Africa. He was a man who we considered a stranger but who didn't consider himself as such. What had made him noticed, in the whole Badiar, was the work he had accomplished during the years while organizing the workers of the fields of rice and peanuts. Besides, he was mentioned countrywide like a model, and his prestige contributed to the development of a vanity that was for him a grant from heaven.

Being a noninsider to the customary secrets, his presence in our convent was considered a serious violation of our customs. Some radicals of the village had wanted to cause a scandal but my father's influence had dissuaded them early on. And yet before entering there, Byllon had made him make particular gestures prescribed by the liturgy of customs. But being a noninsider, these gestures were considered hopeless.

Byllon was happy to have the honor to be in the company of Mr. David Douglas, the one who the whole region appreciated like model. "I come with a man who is not like the others," said Byllon. "This man is called Mr. David Douglas that you have before yourselves. He is an American but of African origin, therefore our brother."

But Mr. David Douglas, with a tone of surprising gravity, handled the situation in an implacable way because for him, nothing serious could come from this simple paroxysm. With his heavy French accent, he didn't have self-conceit to direct proceedings. One of our elders, shocked by the manner that Mr. David Douglas satirized things, addressed Byllon and said to him, in good Peulh Language, "Listen, Byllon, this man is certainly not circumcised. It's a monumental mistake to bring him here."

Suddenly Mr. David Douglas changed his mind and started to look intently at this man who had seriously wounded his state of mind. He rose suddenly and dropped his trousers to exhibit his sex; he faced this disparaging man and said, "Here's mine, where's yours, punk?"

We were all surprised to know that this man not only understood our Peulh Language but was also circumcised, as all of us were. It was a real hurricane of shame that he, imposed on us.. But Mr. David Douglas, satisfied to have raised a challenge that could tarnish his picture, preferred to classify the incident.

Byllon suddenly rose to express himself in these terms: "My brothers, everything that has occurred is only an unhappy incident that teaches us that in spite of all that, in all things it's necessary to know how to keep calm."

Our human society is not only made of men who look alike, who like themselves, and who respect themselves. No, it is also made of the men who don't look alike, who don't understand each other, and who don't like each other.

In spite of it all, each finds its space to live his life.

It's whereas Mr. David Douglas took his speech to assure us of his forgiveness before adding that people always think that Africans don't live in the fullness. But these people, I invite them to come discover the different marvels of the other Africa.

Not the selfish Africa that they describe through reports, where we only see some miserable children with the distended stomachs or the horrors of armed conflicts. There is also another life in society that the Westerners who lived it envy Africa. People are endearing and of a natural simplicity.

Today, said Byllon, I am going to speak to you about something you're not allowed to learn because religion forbids it. But you can know its existence and its misdemeanors nevertheless. It's about the "khortey". His punitive and deadly occult science is often used to punish or to eliminate an enemy. In ancient times, when two adversaries asked at the same time for a girl's hand in marriage (or even in cohabitation), they may have punished themselves or eliminated themselves by this occult science. Two sorts of "khortey exist":

1. Simple khortey, used to shame an enemy or an adversary without killing him. You can use the direction of the wind to throw it from afar toward the targeted person, who falls immediately to urinate and to crap publicly in his trousers while puking a white moss. After it all, if

the author decides to forgive his victim discreetly, he arranges to stop the pain. So after a while, the victim rises in shame with his state of mind injured and his bravery implicated.

2. Wura kadian is a deadly "khortey" used from afar to physically eliminate an enemy. The wura kadian is very dangerous and very difficult to manage. Some prefer to keep it in the bush under the rocks until the day of use. For example, when you throw it against a tree, this one dies and its leaves fall in twenty-four hours.

After all, Mr. David Douglas mocked this history of "khortey", which he didn't believe at all. But Byllon was a man of caste, and as such, he had learned and had possessed the secret since his youth. "Believe me, Mr. David Douglas, before coming out of here, you're going to believe and to respect this history more than any of us," said Byllon.

But Mr. David Douglas always continued his irony.

Byllon left as if he was going outside for some fresh air. Before his return, Mr. Douglas had fallen and urinated and crapped in his trousers. We immediately understood that Byllon had taken the resolution to manage a courtesy lesson to this layman.

When we all awoke, we saw a look frozen on Mr. David Douglas under a deep silence. His first word was to say, "We don't know the deep Africa and we will never know it." All of a sudden, he realized that he had urinated and even crapped in his trousers. What shame? He started shouting loudly. My father realized it and threatened to seriously punish Byllon, but he asked for forgiveness, which was accepted by my father and by Mr. David Douglas.

Strength is, to recognize that Africa was economically poor but culturally rich. The reasons for poverty, we can never say enough, come from a strategy organized by our European colonizers since the time of the big sharing of our African continent between the European powers.

In the different French-speaking, German-speaking, Spanish-speaking, and Portuguese-speaking African countries, the orders were given to direct the following:

- To divide the tribes between them to reign
- To only give their children an elementary teaching in order to use them for the purpose of the colonization
- To give the means to eat while avoiding fattening them
- To make their elites of the small subordinate employees to the wages, not allowing them to become richer
- To create and to maintain a climate of poverty between the colonized so that they stagnate in misery without end
- To avoid allowing the colonized to regroup, otherwise they would become dangerous
- To punish all their revolutionary movements severely so that they obeyed and submitted to the established rule

With these words of order, the only colonized that opted to make the trade were the itinerant "Dioulas" that slipped through between the villages to sell their cheap junk that they received from the Lebanese and Syrian tradesmen, who exercised the trade freely in Africa with the big companies: French, English, and Greek. This Lebanon/Syrian colony had the privileged support of the colonialists in their politics of impoverishment of the African population. Some big foreign companies were based on big profits of these strangers to the detriment of the natives of the continent, who only had the crumbs and were not allowed to bloom economically. In a word, all had been orchestrated to pull the maximum big profits from Africa without truly achieving anything in return for the colonized countries.

It is this poverty initiated by the colonizer countries that continues to impoverish Africa without an international solidarity to put an end to its evolution without enslaving aid conditionality.

In short, Mr. David Douglas, confronted by the mysteries of deep Africa, was haunted by a prophetic dream in which his future in Africa one day appeared to him to be very glorious. He woke up suddenly in the middle of the night, to fall asleep again. When he woke up the morning, all the big notables of the village were united before his hut. When he came outside, all these people greeted him with a very remarkable politeness. Everybody wondered about the shyness of this usually robust character. My father offered him a small stool made of sculpted wood and told him, "Take a seat, my son."

Then he asked him to look at everybody, and said, "All these people came to bless you, and this blessing will protect you against the devil and will bring you permanent happiness during all your life."

Mr. Douglas believed it firmly because the test of yesterday (which no one dared to make allusion to) served him as a lesson. After this ceremony, Mr. Douglas thanked everyone and asked permission to leave the village to go back home. He went to his old car, which finally started after several attempts. The same clouds of black smoke fell over the whole part of the village again. The hubbub of the very deafening motor amused us nevertheless.

When he arrived at home, a messenger came to give him convocation, asking him to present himself in the office of the governor of the region early in the morning. He spent all night long wondering what could be the reason for this convocation.

"Anyway, it could only be friendly, otherwise they would have picked me up in order to carry me to jail," he concluded.

However, he presented himself at the indicated place and hour, and the governor received him with a lot of attention. He congratulated him for a long time before telling him that he was specially invited by the President of the Republic, Supreme Responsible of the Revolution, on the occasion of an official proclamation of the socialist cultural revolution.

Mr. David Douglas wondered how he was going to be able to travel because he worried about the decrepit state of his old car, which didn't seem to be able to face the long road. But the governor suggested that he travel onboard the postal mail truck, which joined the region to the capital. It was a Soviet-made truck, fruit of the Revolutionary cooperation, and moved once per week to the capital.

Two days later, he embarked onboard this truck, and he had the privilege to occupy the cabin place usually reserved for the high dignitaries of the region.

After a day and a half of a laborious journey, he arrived in the capital under a heavy rain. Following the governor's instructions, he was immediately directed to the presidential palace, where he was received and lodged by the authorities like a dignitary.

Three days later, he still hadn't met with the Supreme Responsible of the Revolution, but he always kept in mind that in all circumstances, it's necessary to know how to keep one's blood cold (the wise advice of Byllon, which was henceforth unforgettable to him).

The next morning, a big soldier, exceptionally well-fed and a giant of a giraffe's height, came to tell him in the Malinke language: "The comrade Responsible of the Revolution asked me to drive you to the palace," but Mr. David Douglas didn't understand the language yet. He answered him with his heavy French accent, which is difficult to understand, to politely inform this frightening soldier that he didn't understand Malinke Language and that he was an American. But the soldier immediately retorted, saying, "No, comrade, in this country, the Revolution is global and multiform. Rather you're not a stranger but a Revolutionary comrade, period."

But this soldier's intransigence intrigued him very much and pushed him to take fear. During the jeep ride, he watched everything carefully.

There were placards everywhere with the slogans of the Revolution carrying homage to the Supreme Responsible of the Revolution and its unique political party.

The famished-looking men and women seemed to appear more faithful to the Revolution than trying to survive.

A reddish dust cloud fell over slums, on top of which were arranged blocks of stone to sustain their roofs against the wind. It was the picture of a real poverty in a country rich in mining resources. Mr. David Douglas breathed a sigh all of a sudden, and the soldier driver asked him if all was well; he answered by the affirmative while adding, "The Revolution, that's good, right?"

"Yes, dear comrade, more than you imagine," said the soldier.

Suddenly the jeep turned to the right and started up the Avenue of the Republic, the only one that had not changed its name yet. From there, the number of placards and slogans, and the flag of the country raised along the avenue, increased as they approached the palace.

There were also the different gigantic photos of the Supreme Responsible of the Revolution and those of the big leaders of the International Revolution, such as Lenin, Mao, Castro, and Ché Guevara. In a few minutes the jeep stopped before a post of guards, and the driver, addressed the guards with a mechanical voice, saying, "Ready for the Revolution," and one of the Post Guards, appearing more heedful than the other, asked him, "Your password, comrade militant in uniform?"

Then the driver showed him a special card that identified him as a guard brought closer to the Supreme Responsible of the Revolution, but the Post Guard insisted to have the password nevertheless. Then the driver came down from the jeep to go and discreetly tell him the password, and he congratulated him for his vigilance. The Post Guard raised the gate, and the jeep passed through and parked under a big octogenarian tree and some carefully maintained coconut trees.

He was taken to a big room where there were only military officers. It was the high command, a sort of headquarters that covered the whole country's army, because the Supreme Responsible of the Revolution was also commander-in-chief of the armed forces.

While Mr.David Douglas waited, a superior officer went to announce his arrival. A moment later a plainclothes man from the office of the Supreme Responsible of the Revolution asked him, "Are you Comrade Douglas?"

He said, "Yes, it is I!"

"So come with me," said the man.

As soon as Mr. David Douglas entered in the office, the Supreme Responsible of the Revolution rose to greet him and congratulated him on having cultivated so many quantities of rice. Then he turned toward his close friends sitting around his small office and said to them, speaking of Mr.David Douglas, "Here's a model man who makes our entire people proud. Comrade Douglas is of American origin but today he has become more African than American.

"From nothing, he worked the land to become the best agriculturist of our country. Forsaking the luxury of his native country, he preferred to join the land of his ancestors in the deepest peasantry of our proud nation. He used his scientific knowledge in the domain of agriculture to insure a remarkable success in farming environment. This is the advantage of the use of scientific resources. Here the simple theoretical knowledge is not sufficient.

"The agronomy doesn't consist in assimilating simple theoretical matters, but more in productive practices by the efficient mastery of the land, in the knowledge of the nature, to pull of it the maximum necessary resources to produce man's food and to the development of the society.

"The material basis of our revolution is production.

"It's necessary that this production develops itself, and it's by his development that new openings will be made on new knowledge to which we will be able to reach. Thus, we will be able, progressively, to achieve the legitimate aspirations of which our people are proud and to accelerate, by the same, the system of national construction, the construction of a free, worthy, and responsible Africa that, on the international plan, by its radiance and its contribution, will permit the advent of a new world, presenting itself then, not as simple object, but as active topic, useful to humanity as whole.

"Comrade Douglas demonstrated to us that it's the practice that makes the agronomy, and not the theory. It's why we must dedicate the best of the time to the knowledge of nature, to the analysis of the natural data in order to better orient the practical data when it comes to the development problems facing the nation."

When he finished this speech, one of his government's members made a sign that it was time to join the soccer stadium, where thousands of militants waited for him for the ceremonies of proclamation of the socialist cultural revolution, a historic phase of his craggy power. Before the departure, he required that Mr. David Douglas be dressed in all white, because white is the symbol of his power.

When all was arranged, he joined his car of command followed by many members of his government and some delegates of foreign countries.

He drove himself while his prime minister was seated next to him. Mr. David Douglas and one of the government's members occupied the back seat.

All of a sudden, the serenity was broken when the cortege of official cars headed in the direction of the soccer field under the escort of heavily armed paratroopers and well-dressed bikers. Mr. Douglas appreciated their just values, his moment of glory that he wanted to share with his wife and his children.

Then one could hear traditional musicians sing the praises of the illuminated guide, Supreme Responsible of the Revolution and the unique party.

All along the route, there were crowds who showed their joy and began the words of order of the unique party and the praises of their illuminated guide.

Arriving at the soccer field, the militants collected in jubilation, applauded for the illuminated Supreme Responsible of the Revolution, and wished him long life and health. In a political language sustained by easy words, he started his long speech by which he proclaimed the socialist cultural revolution. He affirmed that the unique party had decided to institute a complete school system that would ensure, through time, the realization of the highest ideals of the supreme goal that the people set to know: To become a united society, evolved, prosperous, worthy, and useful to humanity.

A society completely emancipated, a society responsible for herself, a society dominating her destiny, finally a society rich of one thousand capacities and sovereign in all domains. "We want to change all while changing ourselves at the same time; we want to change the present state of our society qualitatively while enriching ourselves at the same time; in other words, we're determined to promote a concrete revolutionary politics, aiming to the satisfaction of the people's needs, while only living from our own means. It's why the revolution wants the instruction to be at the level of the entire people, that all men and all women, whatever their professions, have the same possibilities to learn and to educate themselves continually. Having taken the determination today to place the school in life, we immediately and automatically modify his measurements while conferring him those of the people.

"We modify the old program at the same time while adapting it to the real imperative of the harmonious and balanced development of the society; this modification entails the stroke of all habits, of all steps capable to have like impacts or consequences to delay the crystallization and the conjugation of our people's progressive wills in search of a united and strong nation.

"We put out a call to all peoples of Africa to which we recall fraternally the big delay that we accuse on the path of history in relation to the peoples that succeeded in conquering and using science, the technique and the technology to be able to arrange today more than material goods and cultural goods than our people.

"The correct appreciation of the present situation of Africa requires a succinct analysis of the previous phases of struggle of our peoples for better conditions of existence and for the defense of their liberty and the African heritage.

"Before the colonial era, Africa was free. With the means existing on her soil, she organized herself, her life, while creating a clean civilization, while inventing her languages, her culture, her writing, her principles of behavior with regard to nature, with regard to man. She built her cities. She always accumulated and transmitted knowledge, more enriched, from generation to generation. In a word, she organized the society according to her own historic realities. As the peoples of all the continents, the peoples of Africa struggled therefore against nature to ensure their collective life. After thousands of years of an existence marked by the self-determination, the auto-administration, the whole responsibility of owning their destiny, from the fifteenth century, the peoples of Africa had contact with Europe, for the misfortune of their continent.

These contacts started with the mediator of the traders who bought, on our coasts, the products such as gold, ivory, and spices.

But it was not about a simple trade, because powerful means of destruction were put at the disposal of these Europeans who came under the cover of this commerce. It succeeded progressively to the imposition of the brutal strength to the peoples of Africa that, contrary to Europe, didn't think of the development of its defensive strengths for the very reason of the socio-political tranquility her people enjoyed, a situation attested to by the historians and the travelers.

But this socio-political tranquility ended, and all Africa, notably black Africa, was reduced to a practice that it never knew: the deportation, to the American continent, between 10 and 20 million Africans were transported; perhaps "of the millions and millions of her children who were going to serve, as beasts, subject to the tax of the size, liable to fatigue duty , in the agricultural exploitations of a kind of capitalism that considered the man of Africa like a simple means of production, a purchasable and marketable merchandise to profit.

"The men, women, and children were linked and deported, in conditions of extreme inhumanity, thousands of miles from their countries and their continent. This hemorrhage, which drained the lifeblood from Africa, provoked a real general unbalance whose catastrophic effects affected in depth all domains of African life: politics, economics, and socio-cultural.

"It's in this state of weakness that the colonial occupation therefore came to fall on our peoples without defense, to weaken them and to exploit them excessively.

"Comrade militants of the revolution, these are the reasons of our poverty.

To finish his speech, he presented to the crowd a few militants who had distinguished themselves by their very remarkable engagement in the revolution, by their action, whose impact positively contributed to the fortifying of the revolution. Among those, there was Mr. David Douglas, who had honor to be appreciated for a long moment by the illuminated guide, Supreme Responsible of the Revolution, and by the crowd.

In the evening, a big artistic and cultural reception took place at the people's palace, an official reception to which Mr. David Douglas was invited. The biggest artists demonstrated their talents, and the theatrical troops performed one after the other. It was indeed a very cultural artistic evening. Mr. Douglas was filled so much with honor that he believed himself on another planet. The beautiful, traditionally dressed girls danced on stage just in front of Mr. Douglas, who occupied the official place.

On this day, his soul was definitely captured by the warm welcome and the generosity of Africans. One day later, Mr. Douglas was given a farm tractor and its accessories.

The governor of the region, who also assisted with the official ceremonies, had understood that henceforth Mr. David Douglas had become a man of respect. He informed him that the Supreme Responsible of the Revolution had given him some firm instructions to look after his well-being, and for this very legitimate reason, he offered to make the journey back home onboard 0f his Soviet-made command jeep while assigning a driver to bring his tractor to the rice fields of Badiar, where he was installed.

Mr. David Douglas, feeling honored, accepted it immediately. Since these moments of glory, he made himself more and more rare in our village. Finally, he moved to the capital and forgot us for good.

When it came to us, the dawn of a new day rose because the difficult tests yielded to a very substantial ease.

People already considered us as full, whole, and responsible men. They didn't treat us as children anymore to initiate the customs and traditions. And the life that was previously a mixture of sadness, absurdity, and hope became for us again full of joy and laughter.

We now walked without supervision. We went to the river and girls, the legendary beauties, waited for us. We were pampered indeed and made the tour of the surrounding villages. I remember Madina Badiar, my village, with emotion; it was a whole universe; it's where I formed my soul of Peulh, of Macina or Macinanké, my under tribe. All seemed possible to me in this life. Anyone who doesn't feel better at home must feel guilty of something, because to me, Madina Badiar was everything for me. The plant perfume, the very shy orange and mango trees, the freshness of water drawn from the semi-deep wells, and the kindness of its inhabitants, testified some with clarity.

Thirsting for knowledge, we constantly asked for Byllon. This is why one night, in the bright moonlight, Byllon united us under a mango tree to speak to us of the domestic responsibility that family's chief, as we were to be called, must assume to really manage his family.

"My brothers," he said, "in one week, you are going to get rid of your white dresses to wear normal dresses. From then on, you will have the right to marry a woman and to become chief of the family. But attention: It's a difficult task. When you marry a woman, to maintain her, it's always necessary, by speech or by action:

- To institute a permanent communication between you.
- To make her smile more often.
- To make her know that you like her more and more.
- To make her know that you have confidence in her.
- To grant her a reasonable space of liberty.
- To make her understand that you have hope for her.
- To share with her all decisions concerning the family.
- To avoid promising her without achieving it.
- To avoid changing behavior or habits to which your wife is already adapted.
- To avoid spying on your wife, to search in her business, or to try to know what she does behind you, because there's an adage that says, the one that looks always ends up finding.

"What you don't know can't hurt you," Byllon continued. "And then, be convinced of a thing; a woman or a man who wants to deceive his spouse has the whole leisure to do it, and nothing or no one can prevent it. Because each is completely free, even the prisoner, the more kept, will know how to benefit from one moment of inattention. Permanent vigilance doesn't exist. If you create a haven of peace in your family, your wife won't want to go elsewhere for the simple reason that no one will want escape happiness.

Also, to choose your wife, you don't look merely for a beautiful girl; you may want a good girl. You don't want an adventure of one evening or some days. You want a steady relationship. Therefore you ripen, then you realize that the essential is beyond the surface and the superficial reports.

In any case, we must respect women, because, certainly, they represent a symbol. It's above all, our mother, and also our sister, our friend, the wife, the mistress. The woman, it's these qualities and it's again well more.

The woman has something in her that makes other women in the street turn to view her passage, to appreciate it. It's not only the men who look at women!

On the other hand, you won't see men turning around to view the passage of another man. It's therefore that the woman deserves a look of particular attention. We live in a visual culture where the women occupy an important place.

It's also her ambivalence, her contradictory, mysterious side that's pleasing; it's her condition of intimate life. The woman, in her complexity, in her diversity, in her unexpected sensation, in her emotions, in her estates of soul, briefly, in what she reflects (her picture), in the way we discern her, we feel her (sensual), dazzled, wild in her pride; in her mystery.

When it comes to the child's education, the parents are all called to provide some efforts in harmony. When the father imposes his rules on the child, the mother must not contradict them, and vice versa. Ever to create the conditions that can bring the child to make the difference between the authority of the father and of the mother. The child is very vulnerable between the ages of five and fifteen years. To scold the child at that moment contributes to traumatize him and seriously affects his intelligence. It's always necessary to communicate with the child, to speak to him and to reassure him of your unconditional affection and to never wound his pride, which is very fragile.

Every human, whatever his age or his social rank, is protected by his pride. Even a baby of one day old is proud. He can cry in anger as he can laugh in joy.

As the spouse, some advice exists to give a good education to the child:

- Speak to the child with words of his mental level.
- Teach the child to trust you and to take you for his confidant; instill in the child good habits.
- Never lie to the child. Do what you say and say what you do.
- Never associate the child with the quarrels of his parents.
- He must always have the idea that his parents are the most perfect in the world.

Help the child to manage his curiosity in the common sense without passing the limit because he's always curious, curious because he doesn't stop asking some questions on everything that interests him. He looks for and wants to know everything. Nothing must escape his questioning.

He likes to test all, to touch, yes, it is it: to see, to touch, to know. Thus, it's necessary to always protect the child from shock and other negative emotions. Anger has a very ominous influence, for example, on the liver, fear on the kidneys. It's not by chance that when someone gets angry, "he sees red or aspen" or that fear "makes one pee on oneself." Many negative things can play on a child's growth. It's necessary to look after the child's health, that's fundamental. Every human being comes to the world carrying his genetic capital. It's a real capital of energy that grows inevitably in him. When it's not there anymore, it's death. So to allow him to last, there's a whole hygiene of life to have. It passes by a balanced diet, assorted physical exercise, controlled breathing, and so on.

Finally, my brothers, we're going to approach a very sensitive topic that gnaws our society by the very complicity of our tradition. It's polygamy. It was certainly a correct and acceptable practice in the past. Nowadays, however, it's not acceptable. Some among us Africans say there are not enough women for men. This last can have five women or more. There're some men who, although married to the church, maintain several other women. In Africa, monogamy is pure hypocrisy, according to a Ugandan poet, because those who proclaim themselves defenders of it always maintain other women without the knowledge of their wives. According to Professor Monica Mweseii of Kenya, polygamy, in modern society in particular, creates many problems, such as the disputes for the meager resources and the lack of transparency of the husbands, contrary to the traditional society, where it was practiced unanimously between the man and the woman. Some researchers affirm that there are more girls than boys, and consider polygamy like a solution to the problem of the unmarried parents. The tendency shows that most people are against polygamy.

However, the theoreticians say that it's more transparent to be polygamous that to pretend to be monogamous while you maintain mistresses and lovers. Of the point of economic view, even the non-Christian finds it very costly.

For the Christian, polygamy is proscribed, and the reason is that God created one woman for Adam. He would have created several if he had accepted it. In several African countries, the woman's barrenness, the fact that a woman gives birth to only one sex, and economic distresses drag men to practice polygamy.

Know that polygamy is an archaic practice and source of several problems in our society. It creates animosity between the wives, and hate spreads to the children. You know, dear brothers, when a woman marries a man, she wants to feel unique, special, and the best of all. When he marries another woman, he makes her feel that she doesn't satisfy him. If a man doesn't want to live with his first wife anymore, because he doesn't find her to his taste anymore or some other reason, he should divorce instead of bringing her a rival.

Disloyalty is an immoral act. Today, man's propensity to disloyalty is more tangible. Some men think the discretion that they insure themselves or the respect that they pretend to have for their wives gives them the right to be disloyal. However, it appears impossible to me to associate respect and disloyalty, disloyalty being itself disrespectful. Does the unfaithful man respect his wife, because he continues to honor her, because he always gives her things that she desires, because he maintains his role of the family's father? No, I really don't think so. The women who are satisfied with this deception at least have an advantage: They're in phase with the reality. On the other hand, there's not any notion of respect toward others in that reality.

Disloyalty is far from being a constructive term. It sends us back to hidden acts that we would not be interested in having publicly disclosed. Can a deceived woman remain proud because she knew how to avoid tensions and storms in her home? Such a woman is definitely a strong person, but is she really happy? The woman, we know it all, when it's about marriage, she gives herself entirely to the person that she loves.

But when another woman appears on scene, this love disintegrates itself gradually and she feels betrayed.

Personally, I don't believe in equality between the man and the woman in love, not that the men don't sincerely like, but they don't risk all, they are not ready to abandon their social situation, their comfort, in the name of love. The women are, as for them, like a well without bottom, filled with love. They give themselves, when they like, to let themselves carried by its ravenous winds that could grind them, to push them to abandon their work, to follow the person they like until the depths of hell. They become, of this fact, a lot more fragile than men in case of separation, since they are without calculation, all in generosity and in grant of oneself.

Respect ensures a good number of elements that harmonize our relations with the other, and we are all okay to look for this harmony.

In short, Byllon closed his intervention with these terms, which this time, again, greatly impressed us.

Without coming back on the different topics already treated by Byllon, it pleases me here to put a particular accent on the fact that women deserve respect and consideration on behalf of the men. They must become aware of the importance of marriage while refusing to yield to the different temptations of life, to respect the woman, who is the mother of humanity, because it is her that, during nine months, endured pains of childbirth to put to the world these popes who represent us before God, these presidents who govern us, these ministers who manage us, these colonels who defend us, these scientists who make for us an even more livable life, these doctors who take care of us every day, and so on.

Today, women are the most devoted in work and of let for account in the different policies of decisions taking. It is necessary that everywhere they affirm themselves .

Although the times are not the same anymore, the reflections of Byllon are stimulating to understand the need to globally and systematically return to importance of the very rich and varied African oral tradition. I'm intimately convinced that by the efforts already provided to save the oral tradition of a Western alienation, this systematic return remains one of the most promising answers to the needs of efficiency for all promoters of the African socio-cultural life.

The imperious needs of formation are added to it, because we won't be able to make anything in a modern world if we know neither how to read nor to write, although it little deprives us to have one past and a perfect knowledge of our own culture.

For a long time, Africa had been considered a barbaric continent, because it does not possess an extensively widespread literary tradition—writing—but an eminent African man of culture said that "writing is the photocopy of the knowledge, but she's not the knowledge himself." However, the current interest is to rebuild what we lost by the race of our own history.

When Byllon left us in the middle of the night, we realized that he had not mentioned sexuality, which was for us a very important topic. Teenagers that we were, we didn't have any experience thereon. The next day, we hastened to attract his attention on that, and he promised us to come back to speak to us on this taboo topic.

Unfortunately, he could not make it before the end of our stay in the convent. However, according to Bernard BANGA of the African Magazine "AMINA" on the medical subject, " sex is beneficial for health because it's a source of pleasure, it removes depression, and it decreases anxiety. The pleasure of the orgasm gives energy and an incontestable feeling of well-being. Regular sexual activity could increase life expectancy! To the inverse, is prolonged abstinence ominous?

"No, since sexuality is not an absolutely vital need such as to eat, to drink, or to sleep. "However, prolonged abstinence can be a source of frustration and can drag psychological reactions such as jumpiness and fretfulness.

"Does making love during pregnancy increase the risk of miscarriage? No, miscarriages are frequent accidents: One woman out of three makes one in her life. This occurs most of the time during the first quarter of pregnancy, and is almost always due to an anomaly of the egg. In any case, sexual intercourse, even vigorous, is never the reason. In the second quarter, it's rare that a pregnancy is interrupted. Finally, for a long time we thought that sexual intercourse could encourage premature childbirth in the third quarter because, at the time of the orgasm, it provoked uterine contractions. Actually, it's proven today that's not the case. It's rare that a physician must counsel to abstain of sexual intercourse at the end of pregnancy.

Is there a tie between sexual intercourse and urinary infections in the woman?

"Urinary infections or post-coitus cystitis exist. Why?

"During sexual intercourse, the feminine urethra of about three centimeters that leaves from the bladder and descends into the urinary opening is very opened. "Besides, the micro trauma that this small channel undergoes encourages the ascent of the bacteria present in the vulva region, and therefore results in urinary infections. But women who are subject to many infections have an efficient, preventive solution: It's to urinate soon after sexual intercourse.

Is it advised against having sexual intercourse during a woman's period?

No, from a medical point of view, there's not any reason, if one chooses not to abstain from the sexual act during this time. It doesn't increase the bleeding or provoke an inflammation, since the blood of the periods comes from the mucous membrane of the uterus. Only reserve: During this time, there is greater risk to contract a sexually transferable infection, of the man toward the woman or the inverse, because with blood, the transmission of the germs is done more easily.

And then, let's remember, even during the periods, the starting up of a pregnancy is not impossible in the absence of contraception.

Also, the condom does not prevent all sexually transferred diseases. Sure thing, it has been demonstrated for a long time in the laboratory that the condom will not pass the virus of AIDS, and the studies of couples where one is HIV positive, and the other is HIV negative, confirm this remarkable efficiency. The condom protects well against transferable bacterial infections, for example chlamydeous and gonorrhea. But viral infections, such as herpes, papilla virus, or those that provoke genital warts, can get settled almost everywhere on the genital sphere. And there, the condom protects the sex itself, but not close by.

Is a sex life possible after heart problems?

Yes, the cardiac risks bound to the activity in lovemaking are most modest. Usually, after an infarction, the medical "green light" for the resumption of sexual activity is given when the patient returns home: Physicians consider a reference mark the ability to walk up two flights of stairs without symptoms. Physicians don't usually forbid sexual activity, except when the heart is very tired. But then all physical effort, even light, is forbidden.

Can one transmit a vaginal mycosis to her spouse?

The experts say no. A vaginal mycosis occurs when the flora of the vagina is unbalanced, following a too aggressive hygiene or the taking of antibiotics. In this case, the *Candida albicans*, mushrooms normally present in the vagina, develop in an excessive way. But the penis defends itself perfectly against these germs except for in diabetic men, who are more subject to the infections, because their defenses are lessened. Today, these mycoses are not considered like sexually transferable infections. For women, pain during sexual intercourse has various reasons.

Yes, pain at the time of penetration can be due to an insufficient lubrication of the vagina, to an infection, or to a vaginal mycosis. Those felt more deeply in the bottom of the vagina or in the underbelly can be provoked by an inflammatory infection to the level of the horns, by endometriosis, or by proliferation of the uterine mucous membrane on the neighboring organs. In any case, it's necessary to speak of this problem to one's physician, in order to get diagnosis and treatment.

Can lack of an erection be caused by an illness?

Yes, some studies even show that these lack of erection , frequent enough for men of forty years or more, can permit one to discover an unknown underlying illness, in a precocious way. It's the case of one man out of three. How is this possible?

The arteries of the verge can, as with other arteries, get clogged. And as they are among the narrowest of the human body, they can be among the first to choke, notably at the time of a hypertension, of an excess of cholesterol, of diabetes, or of tobacco addiction. A man concerned about penile erection has two good reasons to go for a consult: first to do a cardiovascular health balance with an eye toward prevention; then, because some treatments exist to recover sexuality in full bloom.

Does menopause have an impact on sexuality?

Yes and no. After fifty years, a good number of women keep up a satisfactory sex life, without medical help necessary. For others, menopause comes with annoyances due to a hormonal deficiency. The most frequent complaint is vaginal drought, which decreases pleasure or even makes sexual intercourse unpleasant.

If a substitutive hormonal treatment is prescribed, it largely resolves these problems. Otherwise, some local application of vaginal lubricants is possible, as frosts – without hormones, and without contra-indications – over-the-counter in the pharmacy. If their action proves to be insufficient, the physician can prescribe creams or vaginal ovum on the basis of the hormone estrogen. These treatments give back to the mucous membrane vaginal suppleness and humidity. Not passing or little in the blood circulation, they have few side effects."

These villagers' vigils to the fattening pond of the moon, and to the heart of the tropics, teach customs and civilizations from generations to generations.

Thanks to the oral tradition that continues to play its role of vector of the universal civilization. In spite of the real advent of the book and the use of reading, in the current sense of the term, the oral tradition continues to resist the risks of scientific and technological progress.

The development of the book in a society or in a country is simply a function of the need to read by the population. However, these needs are not motivated, stimulated, and maintained by the abundance or the quality of the available literature. While the oral tradition transmits itself unconditionally from generations to generations.

In West Africa, a respectable literature always existed before the arrival of the Europeans. It was nearly exclusively dominated by the "masters of the speech" (Griots, traditional storytellers). And in some regions, such as the Loma country, in Guinea, a very functional alphabet existed of which the radiance, yet real, remains little known or, frankly, unknown.

Oral literature had a precise mission, during this period, that some present as merely barbaric. The main elements of its role were to sustain musical realizations, to praise the exploits of the king or heroes, to praise kindness and good conduct, and to disapprove of the incompatible attitudes in place with moral principles, rules, and social traditions. In other words, even under this shape, literature was a stimulant of weight and a sure vehicle for the culture, for the promotion of civilizations, of which we will always regret the abrupt stoppage of the development process.

Today, oral character doesn't have this eminent role, with the introduction of writing.

It was not until two o'clock in the morning that we fell asleep. In spite of it all, we woke up very early to allow the tailor of the village, who had already arrived, to take our measurements individually in order to prepare new dresses that we must wear to the ceremonies of the end of our initiation.

As soon as we finished, our Baho hurled us down deliberately, to reassure himself that we had all mastered what we learned. For example, it was prohibited for us to lose or forget our objects, to speak while eating, to let the grains of rice fall while eating (otherwise, they make you collect them by mouth), to rise before the common dish was finished, to go to the toilet, to urinate without washing the hands, and so on.

We left therefore in the morning to surrender to the river. I had forgotten my "Nghodhorkun," a small sculpted stick with which I had to punish the uncircumcised every time I met them on the road. It also protected me against the bad minds, according to the dedicated rituals.

Our Baho noted this infringement without attracting our attention, and he put my "Nghodhorkun" in his pocket. . Before arriving at our destination, he made himself a big liana whip.

We immediately felt that this excursion was not going to be restful for us. We were sad and very anxious because we were absolutely sure that this whip was destined for us. Our enthusiasm faded, and the attitude of our Baho became more and more strange. When we arrived at our destination, our Baho asked us to empty our pockets and to deposit their contents before him. It was at that moment that I realized that I had forgotten this cursed small piece of wood. All my mates executed themselves perfectly, but I was shaking and I looked at the sky as if I waited for a miracle to save me. Suddenly, he challenged me, asking me, "What are you waiting for?"

Shivering with fear, I started stuttering to him because confessing my mistake was not easy thing for me to do.

"I'm waiting for you; know that my patience won't hold for a long time," he said.

Soon I realized that I didn't have any loophole and that it was necessary to risk and say the truth because his anger was at its height. I should tell him that I had forgotten my "Nghodhorkun".

He looked at me for some minutes without diverting his eyes to express his disappointment and his surprise. "I expected someone else to commit such silliness but not you," he said.

I blushed and whimpered discreetly. Holding the whip with his left hand, he ordered me to undress and to get on my knees, a thing that I hesitated to do, and I implored him constantly to forgive me but he didn't want to hear anything. My slowness angered him more and drove him to catch me and undress me by force. Before his anger and his impatience, I got on my knees without calculation while constantly asking for forgiveness, but he attacked me with a fillip on my back, and I felt the pain throughout my entire body. My mates, shared between the fear and the sadness, observed the scene with a lot of bitterness. This day, these moments and this place were for me an unforgettable childhood memory. After having finished beating me up twelve fillips, he returned this cursed sculpted small stick that caused me so much worry and pain.

Between the chaos and the silence, I believed at that moment that I lived a plain life, one of a reduced person treated like a beast of burden and deprived of most elementary rights. I told myself, anyway, soon I would succeed in emancipating myself from the psychological weights of my present condition. The truth is that our Baho was a calm man but authoritative. He could lose temper at any time without any obvious reason and could spend his time dictating his rules of conduct to us. After all, he seemed to regret a little having hit me so hard.

He tried to justify himself by telling us, "Listen to me, my brothers; it's useless to insist, people will never be what we want them to be. We can always try, but they won't change much. The truth is that we support critics with difficulty even if it constricts our happiness."

After my punishment, we began a long walk in the forest in the company of a dog named Kalbhou, very sociable and very well trained for hunting. We pursued our walk in border of a relief characterized by the presence of a mountain chain paved in the shape of a belt, dominated by the very famous Mount Badiar, which spread from the north (Sambailo) to the west (Sareboido) of which the whole left superior constituted the tray of Mount Badiar, very favorable to tourism because of its fauna and its very rich and varied flora.

In this, the beginning of the rainy season, the storms threatened and obliged us at times to interrupt our walk, and the entire landscape that ignites and dies out failed to divert us from our objective, but our determination to reach the Koliba stream was nevertheless irreversible. Soon we were at a clearing at the Sarekaly Village.

We were no sooner away from it that the silence fell again. The silence and the dust were the picture of this village of gray earthen huts, between Sareboido and the Koliba stream, Old men sat to the dry shade. "Twenty years ago," recalled our Baho, "all was green. It's the drought that changed everything. What is going to become of these people?"

These were not nomads, they don't have the wandering habit. In the past, because of rains (July and August), the men even fished on the plains. Today, all that remains is the sand stolen by the wind. Crushing heat, just some occasional wells, and the villages of Altou and Alkeme on these stones seats are all that survives.

Here we're very close to the Koliba stream. The small village of Bowebhe, home of a cows breeder tribe, welcomed us heartily because it's there that our Baho was born. In ancient times, this was one of the big prosperous cities of our region, a prosperity that owed lot to its riparian position on the Koliba stream. This village is distinguished by its white walls in the shade of the big trees, and the stream at the head of the street. The children played, the women washed the linen, and the men raised the nets. The stream, again and always, was the center of life. It's hardly an hour after noon, and the herds came to drink. Straw huts dominated the bank. Temporary camps became permanent by the race of history. Its inhabitants are two tribes, the Bowebhey and the Kinsibhey, which look alike. They come from Kaadey in the region of Gaoual.

This stream is just as important and vital for the nomads as for the sedentary, as vital for the cows breeder as for the fisher; this lets me believe that only water gives a sense to the landscape. It was in this very welcoming village that we spent the night. The ambiance, honors, and pastoral music to the fattening pond of the moon made me forget my twelve fillips.

Early the morning, they came with us very close to the stream, to show us the place where fishers "Somonoh" dry and smoke the freshwater fish, in the herbs and the woods of "Lookhun" and the dugout slips on the ideal mirror of water. We watched the flight of birds, heard the screams of children, and saw the slow gestures of the fishers who threw the sparrow hawk.

Two short hours by dugout, we joined Sarewuro, a bank eaten by high herbs, some gardens on the border of the stream, and the village bank, where fish are treated to be sold to the local market of Sareboido, even to the big market of conakry the capital.. The fishing season is July and August. More than one thousand come to work here, explained Demba Boiro, our guide, of the Guinean, of the Senegalese, of the Bissau-Guineans.

Besides, it's the same people who own the shops and the dugouts. Fishers, nomadic "Thyouballos," they often come from the riparian villages of the Tyayanga stream that waters the plains of Missira, Foulamansa, and Pakaye.

It's the drought that causes the need to move and to be going to look for water, food, grazing, farther away, always farther away.

In some weeks, rains are going to come back abundantly; we already feel it in this heaviness of air, this impression of imminent storm. Deliverance, the hope that the Earth is going to be able to nourish itself, that rice and corn will be scattered. As Demba Boiro told it, for a long time we refused to admit that the western part of our region was threatened by the drought. It had a miserable connotation.

Today, with this same drought increasing, it posed the same problems as elsewhere. For example, the relations between nomadic and sedentary, the fear of the other, of its sorcery, these were signs!

In the meantime, the hot wind reigns over the landscape, blowing in from the neighboring Sahara. In spite of it all, the rainfall of the moment announced the imminence of the season of the big rains.

As soon as we finished our visit, we saw ourselves offered gifts: dried fish and meat. We were filled with joy and constantly thanked them.

Demba Boiro came with us by dugout to the village to say goodbye to our hosts but out of the village, our Baho provided us with another program.

Our Baho told us, "I was born close to here, within two miles, more or less; would you like to visit the place?"

Without discussing it, we took the road leading east of the village. Suddenly, he turned left on a path. "Follow me," he said.

We jogged there within a few minutes. Finally, he stopped on a sort of empty lot surrounded by a shrunken beach. A few yards farther, behind a rocky embankment, we hear the rushing water of the Koliba stream. The soil was sandy. Here and there were some old foundations of cement. Sometimes the tiles, the rotted joists, and some gray and black boards formed heaps of rubble on the former site of the houses. The grass, the brambles, and young trees grew all around it. A true ghost town! When we speak of ghost town, we always think about those of the desolate American West where the air is so dry that a hundred years after the departure of the last inhabitant, the shutters creak again at the windows.

Here the elements were a little more aggressive. It had left only a few remains of this village. A little amused, I asked, "Is it here that you were born?"

Our Baho looked at me, smiling. He was very proud to the bottom to be one of the last representatives of another age. He showed me a periphery made of cement that hardly emerged through the soil.

"Yes, my dear, it was here! My father had a piece of land on the other side of the stream. If we can call that the land!"

What ungrateful country! Beside, there's not even one farmer for miles around. It became a place of tourism, and I believe it's better that way. These poor peasants killed themselves working and hardly succeeded in feeding themselves.

He put his thumbs in the reverse of his worn-out jacket and began to walk along the former big street. "It was the road to Sareboido back in the day," he said while turning around toward me. It took the whole day to go from here to Sareboido.

When we were almost outside of the village, our Baho continued to walk.

Then we arrived before the skeletal remains of a truck abandoned since the colonial times. The rusty remains rested on a pad of cement, standing as tall as a man and difficult to reach. Behind this truck was a formless heap of blackish boards invaded with nettles and thistles. Our Baho looked dreamily at all it.

Suddenly Demba Boiro told us, "Hey, my dear brothers, I come with you up to here, and I'm going to return to attend to my business. Thank you for everything that you have done for us."

"It's indeed very kind on your part," said our Baho.

As soon as he tried to leave us, Kalbhu the dog began to follow him. It was necessary to restrain him. He was very unhappy and barked loudly. He had indeed fallen in love with Demba Boiro, who had granted him particular attention.

We got back on the path, loaded with smoked fish, dried bush meat, and living chickens. All of the gifts, without doubt, illustrated the African fraternity. At every village that we passed, men and women watched us pass and sang for us without speaking to us; it's the custom. Personally, I could not imagine that people adored us in this way. We got round the village of Sareboido to pick up the small side road that appeared, which permitted us to climb the mountain and to come down again very close to the Lombol River, close to our village.

There we quenched our thirst and took a rest for more than an hour before continuing our path. From the river, we could hear the young men and the girls singing melodiously while returning to the village after a day of work.

Aliou Ndongo, who became my uncle-in-law, sang the "Kerona's" songs with his unique voice. It was six o'clock in the evening when we entered our village, Madina Badiar.

Our arrival attracted a curious throng of sympathizers to discover the contents of our luggage. We were pampered like small princes; our cousins teased us. Suddenly, our dinner was deposited, and the crowd fell apart immediately to allow us to eat and to take a rest. Here we were, within five days of the big ceremony marking the end of our thirty days of initiation. The things moved fast and our shopping constantly increased.

Very early the morning, we went to the bush to harvest the grains of palm to act as an ingredient to the multiple meals that will be prepared for the ceremony. Mbouna the Koniagui and Samba Sidibe came with us. These two men were ready to brave all dangers to satisfy our need. Here we are at the foot of a palm tree about thirty meters high. This gigantic tree of the hot regions, from its stark, naked, and rough stem, to its big fanlike leaves, produced red oil from its seeds.

Mbouna climbed the tree first. Here, his life rested on a fine liana belt, the "wakkawol." After a long and terrifying ascension, Mbouna was attacked by swarms of flies that whirled around him. He attempted to mark the area of palm in vain. He was obliged therefore to come down again. From there, began a real wandering in search of palm seeds.

On the road, a woman sang the exploits of a valorous hunter who triumphed once over a lion. Samba gave her a courtesy gesture but the woman didn't stop singing; she continued on the road. I told myself internally that one day on the same path, God willing, another woman would sing a history illustrating my own bravura; all is possible in life, I thought. For the clan of Mbouna, the Koniaguis, all activity in the bush touched the domain of "Dyalan," the mind consecrated of the place. M'Bouna prostrated then under an octogenarian tree and pronounced some incantations to communicate with the soul of his ancestors, then stood up to tell us, "Let's go, all will go well."

Soon he went back up a gigantic palm tree. There he cut several branches before reaching the regimes of palm; it was indeed difficult and tiring work. Sometimes the exhausted men inadvertently cut their liana belt and fall like a rock. To die for a regime of palm is also the fate of the villagers.

The efforts of Mbouna were rewarded; he harvested several stands of palm. After having passed long hours suspended in the emptiness, Mbouna finally descended to the ground.

Climbing again to more than thirty-five meters, Mbouna wandered about to discover several more stands of palm. Swinging on the palm, this extraordinary climber dominated the whole vegetation like a sparrow hawk pierced to his biggest height of skimming. His face expressed an astonishing calmness. Here the least mistake would be fatal. This past year, the biggest harvester of our village died. The liana belt that held him gave out. Some meters from there, Samba Sidibe, unconscious of the danger, tried to climb another palm tree without using the liana belt, but he could not go to the end of this oppressive innocence.

During this time, at the foot of the tree, each of us held his breath. At the same time, we observed Mbouna working because, in Africa, the young steal the secrets of the ancients while observing them and while imitating them.

This harvest of palm constitutes a crucial phase of our initiation, although we freed the essential stage of our initiation. We don't really feel ready to climb such heights.

Mbouna and Samba Sidibe are assigned the transport of the whole harvest to the Sankabhé, a clan specialized in extraction of palm oil. After two days, we are going to recover our well-refined oil, ready for consumption.

From February to April, when rains make themselves very rare and the tropical sun runs the temperatures up into the hundreds in the shade, the Sankabhé, with their wives and their children, come to get settled around our village, very close to Lombol River, for the harvest of palm oil. The Sankabhé women work as hard as the men because they are charged with the extraction of the palm oil.

Early in the morning, they utter screams of incantation, implore God the all powerful so that he protects their men who left early for the harvest of palm seeds. The Sankabhé men show the children how to harvest palm seeds. To find a palm carrier of seeds in full maturity, one must watch the air to see the stands of palm, the rest watch the foot of the palm because the seeds always fall on the ground when they are in advanced maturity. It's necessary for the clan of Sankabhé not to be afraid to climb all the way to the top of the palms. Samba Sidibe and Mbouna are only amateurs and do not belong to the clan of Sankabhé. At the Peulhs, the harvest of palm seeds is not a main activity and must not be forced. It's the man who decides, and only he knows when it's necessary to go there.

We were at the end of the thirty days of wandering between two worlds, the one of the child that is past and the one of the man who we hope to become.

On the next-to-last day of our initiation, we did the warrior's walk in the company of our elders. We bordered the strands of the shade facing the fields of the Badiaranké, redoubtable warriors. We finally discovered the places that mark our people's history. Other times, the slave traders came to hide here to wait for passersby. It's there that the brave Samba Dannah, big war chief, faced them one day.

In spite of our young age, we now know our people's history. We started the ultimate phase of our initiation then. During our course of initiation, we essentially ate meat and drank milk in order to create the conditions of our rebirth as adults. For us, the Peulh, meat and milk represent the two vital foods of our existence.

Back in the village, the young girls and boys danced for us.. . Everybody in the village was proud to sustain us. The men and the women treated us well.

The drums and the pastoral flute approached the scene of the nocturnal ritual dance that gathered all people. Joy and the tenderness that surrounded us momentarily swept away the dark and challenging day of our circumcision. In our honor, the girls made themselves as beautiful as flowers. By their songs and by their dances, they started the rituals of seduction, proving their devotion thus to their future spouses. For them, this ritual dance also constituted an initiation. Since nightfall, everybody had assembled at the places of ceremony chosen by the old. This place possessed an entry and a symbolic exit. The guests arrived by hundreds from all parts. The announcement of the end of our initiation propagated itself in the surrounding villages as if by magic. Before joining the crowd, we accomplished a secret ritual during which a restricted circle of our elders surrounded us to help free us of our adolescence and to take control of ourselves.

Finally, naked as the day we were born, we washed with milk. This gesture symbolized the physical act of the conception and initiation rebirth. Now we were ready to face the early morning, the ultimate stage of our initiation. The big moment was approaching, when the elders began their incantations, and we were under way for the dance.

There, we had to dance, to jump, and to laugh to show that we're healed and that nothing goes more badly and also to erase definitely the child that sleeps in all of us and to give birth to the adult. It's what we have made until the morning. In our man's life, it was the first morning of the world.

Along the way, an enlivened crowd hurried to join us to form a famous human effervescence. The guests fully regained the small places that were reserved for them. One could hardly see our amused girlfriends, who waited behind the crowd. The places were overcrowded, and all alleys were black with people; it was a real human swamp of jubilation. We breathed cool air, and one gave us some accolades as if we had come back from afar. The attractions were numerous: the magicians, the Griots, and the music; the children didn't know where to poke their heads.

Suddenly, the main orchestra began to play and dedicate the most popular song, "The Champatché." Soon the whole crowd scorched? itself: We sang, we danced, we laughed, and the one who had the proudest pace became the one who came to see the spectacle of the other, and to give oneself in spectacle. The boys threw supported looks, the girls pretended to ignore them , but donned their most beautiful clothes. The scarf became a tool of seduction that the girls placed around the neck of the boy who she liked to avail him of her loving attention: the different cloths, to the bright colors are arranged learnedly to enhance the drawing of the face. On the other hand, under the orange trees, the tourbillion lulled and the lawns were sparse, the fatter grass; I took a little breath and debated some instances with my friends; it was for me an unforgettable moment of my life because that day, the life that had been a mixture of sadness become again one of joy and laughter. The Griots of the village, these real possessors of the history chair, attached to the oral tradition and their native land, made us more inexhaustible praises.

All clans had come: The hunters, the sinners, the blacksmiths, and the weavers all wanted to represent themselves. The hunters danced clothed of their hunt dresses and vainly waved their empty or loaded rifles, who knows? Anyway, the ambiance was at its height. The whole village was filled with screams of joy.

My girlfriend, Niang Mariam, took a small chance to seduce me. When I spoke to her, she only smiled at me while fixing me with her eyes. She had three assets to seduce me: Her looks, this look of fire that consumed more than one. Her smile made of innocence that was one truth trap for the predators who are the men. The parts of her body that seduced me more were naturally her eyes, her mouth, her power, and her buttocks. From that moment, I understood that seduction was very important for a woman who wants to make herself liked. As she could not sweep the man herself, she had to learn to seduce the man by her smile, her cleanliness, and her availability, also by her beauty and by the cultural diversity, so much on the culinary plan that sartorial.

For African women, all is made to seduce the man. Her strength to seduce resides in her manner of dress, her walk, her speech.

At five o'clock in the evening, she's already home to receive her husband. The house is already cleaned, a good odor cleared itself of it, and she wears a light and sensual dress. After the husband takes a rest for some minutes, she joins him to wash his feet and to massage him, while asking him for news of the day. It's necessary to say that she always prepares in advance the clothes that her husband will wear the following day. The woman, the wife, especially values her husband's wardrobe. Food or the moment of meal is also an opportunity of seduction for the African woman. The table or the raffia rug is always prepared well, with a clean tablecloth, colorful dishes, and quality. The presentation of the table must give one the desire to eat. The woman always takes the first gulp. During the meal, she gives him the best pieces of fish or meat. She often puts some pieces of food in his mouth like a mom and her baby. In any case, she constantly removes the bones from fish before giving it to her husband. To give a constant vigor to her man, the food is often spiced or peppery or contains other aphrodisiac elements.

It's in the bedroom that the seduction of the African occurs a lot. For the African woman, the room must always smell good. The odor of incense is one of the elements to charm the husband. In the room well decorated by pictures, one must listen to music distributed with a resonant bass. One must find pots of flowers. The man must have jars of pearls or erotic feminine clothes spread on a small table. The sheets are changed every day. The African woman knows how to marry the colors and decor of the dresses that seduce a lot. One will find some bracelets on her arms, a chain on her neck, or simple shoes that seduce. The hairdressing also plays an important role in her manner to seduce. She has the respect, the affection, and a lot of patience with her man. For her the man is the key of her paradise, how to put him at ease and in all situations that allow him to be happy. How does a respected and pampered man put all at the disposal of his wife?

When the man swims in happiness, he deposits gold under his wife's feet. One also speaks a lot of the legendary smile of the African woman. She's rarely angry. Ever since childhood she has been taught to smile, to sit down. The whole society participates in the girl's education. One constantly tells her what she must do or mustn't do. To observe her mother in the home is the best practice for her. I don't want to come back to the problem of sexuality, but I confess that an African woman in a room with her man is something! Her pearls around the waist, her small loincloths, her affectionate fingers, the odor of her body, her bracelets can only make the African woman the most attractive and bewitching.

My girlfriend Niang Mariam was predestined to all these woman's qualities. In her heart my place always existed, but that day this existence affirmed itself more. She placed her scarf around my neck and invited me to dance with her. I hesitated again to tell her my feelings of worship and pure love because my man's liberty was still limited by the customs. Nevertheless, my guilty look was full of message of love expressions that she did not find difficult to read so much that they were clean and omnipresent. Our lasting looks crossed themselves all night long constantly, like two equal weights in a balance.

Dawn illuminated without me realizing it, and the latest stage of our initiation announced itself so quickly that I felt cheated concerning time, the ambiance was so livable to me. Suddenly the pastoral song that could only be sung in that similar circumstance was begun by an old man to indicate the imminence of our departure for the sacred place in the bush. We immediately regrouped but it was necessary to wait for the end of this song, which allowed us to leave. This long song was made of the pastoral poems of our corpus collected by our ancestors.

The Peulhs continue to keep intact the nearly millennial traditions of our ancestors that have descended of the valley of the Nile. The pastoral life of the Peulhs includes a set of magic practices that expresses itself through rituals, one life-style bound to their pastoral activities. Their vision of the world, their conception of life, their passion for the raising of beef appears spoken through so-called pastoral poems and acts. The breeder Peulh deeply believes the virtue of the words, of the force and the efficiency of speech, thinks to master and to domesticate the occult strengths by symbols, rituals, and magic formulas. For the pastoral Peulh, the geniuses when the malevolent minds try to harm his children, his wives, and his beef, it's necessary to implore their action while constantly making recourse to magic incantations. That making, he thinks to protect them in case of illness.

Finally, the song finished, we were again under way. The day was not yet dawned. On the savanna drowned of shade, just a gleam that drags, one can hear the scream of unknown animals, of monkeys who sneer, of birds that bicker. Our last stage was to take the early track and to penetrate in this wild shrine. But what happiness on this dawn of the first day of our passage to the adult age!

The sun was going to topple over the hill. The savanna took a tinge of gold. It's hardly six o'clock in the morning, and on the track, herds of beef raised a cloud of dust. It was indeed the dream of Africa. Here we were in a place held secret, a lake that contained blessed hot and sacred water. Here we washed a new time. This famous ritual purification celebrated today our passage to the adult age. All of our elders were here to help us. Each of us was naked and induced of natural cocoa butter then crouched down on an immaculate sheepskin. Our elders turned us around, pronouncing some incantations, then abandoned us under the hot sun for one hour, during which we were washed and drank this blessed water. Later our elders, armed with liana whips, lined up in two orderly parallel lines between which we must pass one by one while running.

According to the tradition, these elders must whip us during our passage neither without crying nor to be reticent. We must implore the punishment to prove our bravery and our faculty to pass to the adult age. The one who passes and supports the pain will have succeeded and will make a decisive step toward his manly destiny. But the one who cries in pain will have failed the test and will face all his life the misfortune; he will be tyrannized by his clan, and he will have difficulty finding a woman. Sometimes it happens that an adult who kept a hatred of you since your adolescence, because of one of your disrespectful acts, that even you have forgotten, takes advantage of the opportunity to take revenge and whip you heartily.

At the end of the two ranks, a group of adults waited us to stretch us our new adult dress. I was the first to pass the test; when one called me, my heart beat but my determination was very strong. I took off like a wounded panther and ran while passing between the whips. After having passed this infernal punishment, I sat before the adults, who stretched me my new adult dress, and I dressed very quickly. These people congratulated me but my eyes, red and nearly weepy, could not hide the pain that gnawed my entire body. Fortunately, all my mates could endure this suffering without crying.

After having finished getting into our adult dress, it was necessary to fire five gunshots to indicate to the people of the village that all five of us succeeded in passing the latest test at the end of our initiation; but in these sacred places that symbolize nonviolence, firing a gunshot was prohibited. It's only along the way that the five shots are fired.

While hearing these shots, all people of the village shouted with joy while thanking God, the all powerful, and while blessing us from the bottom of their heart. That day, my village appeared to me even more resplendent. Madina Badiar, this prestigious and surprising village to the very shy orange trees, is the cradle of the history of the Badiar, the soul of a region of more than 500,000 inhabitants. The more one goes up northwards, the more there's mountains in the far and always as many beautiful villages. My village, with its huts newly redone in yellow straw, is astonishingly beautiful in summer when the sky is low and gray. One speaks a lot of the heat of summer but in this village, one feels it very little because of the greenery. That's to say that the feast was held under a perfect temperature with some clouds on the Badiar mountainous landscapes where the nature lovers can find their account, considering its spaces and in more, if one likes to relax indeed.

Become henceforth adults, we were obliged to ask the dean of the village for permission to enter, to settle and to live in his traditional territory. While we waited around the village, our elders sent a messenger accompanied by a Griot to the dean of the village. Once arrived, the Griot started a sort of historic narration of the events, which was a witness during several decades, this old man with the wrinkled face, the white hair, and the long beard. This old man was a little sensitive to flatteries and seemed worn out by the exaggeration of the Griot, and with his local fan that he held by the right hand, he gestured to them to sit down.

It was then the messenger expressed himself in these terms: "Oh! The man who lived more days than everybody in this village, blessed by God, the all powerful, it's you only that is the depository of the secrets of this village, it's you that I address and permit me to deliver you a message of which I'm the carrier. Five of our children became brilliantly adult by the virtues of the rituals and traditions consecrated while undergoing thirty days of initiation, sent me to transmit you their respectful greetings and to ask you to accept their adherence to the circle of the adults in order to benefit not only from your protection and blessing but also of the advantages and inconveniences bound to adult's life in your village."

"Is it this kind of message of which you're the carrier?" asked the old man.

"Yes, it's exact," answered the messenger.

"In this village, I'm the dean," said the old man. "They can enter. I wish them welcome because they're only our children who pass a stage of their life to another; however, tell them that in this village, violence, stealing, indiscretion, lies, and adultery are rigorously forbidden."

Before leaving, the Griot addressed its praises to the dean in these terms: " "Oh Mawdho Missidhé! Glory, longevity, and health of iron to you that protect us and always directed us toward the right path. May the all powerful continue to watch over you and on your entire people". "Thank you and may God guide your steps," exclaimed the dean."

Left satisfied, the messenger and his companion called on some musicians, notably the singers and the violinists. These musicians began their songs through which they wished to welcome us to the village. Suddenly, they were interrupted by the messenger who took the floor to tell us in a high voice that the dean of the village received our message and wished us welcome in his traditional territory in which, however, violence, stealing, indiscretion, lies, and adultery are rigorously forbidden.

Without wasting our time, we started our triumphal entry in the village. The music, the applause of one and the other, caused strident echoes through the whole village. We walked as invincible warriors, full of vigor and pride. In the overflowing crowd, we paved ourselves a passage. Arriving at the ceremony, we found a place especially arranged for us. This little overhanging place was covered entirely with immaculate beef skins. As soon as we sat down, silence reigned. A long speech was going to begin. The dean of the village used the speech to thank everybody and declared according to the tradition that the period of our initiation finally reached its end and that we were now adults capable of founding and directing our own family. Soon after this speech, all old people left to allow the time to the young who wanted to have more fun.

We continued the feast although the lighting of the moon yielded to clouds in prelude to the rains season. We danced and we laughed with our girlfriends, who surrounded us lovingly. Some crowds formed themselves by youngsters who sometimes harassed the girls by fruitless declarations of love. In spite of it all, the atmosphere was very restful and didn't lead to any misunderstanding. Our Baho made us a sad farewell while individually giving us good advice. Since that night, I never saw him again. The crowd dispersed itself gradually, and at dawn, only the respective members of our families remained, and our girlfriends, who fought against the sleepiness that constantly overwhelmed them. The more dawn illuminated the horizon, the more our ardor gave up to a fatigue generated by two days of insomnia and uninterrupted uproar.

Each of our families persisted in recovering its bowls used to serve the hosts. All was finished now, and each of us was free to join his family or to go where he wanted. However, my friends and I believed we had become inseparable without knowing that the destiny reserved us quite the opposite.

During several days, we walked together to do the usual greetings in manner of thanks to the families who appeared supportive in our place. Day after day, we were invited to the table of life for the big feast of the existence. We let ourselves drag gracefully as if we had just been taken from our mother's stomach and as if our greatly open eyes never touched lightly the sadness. I knew that my mates and I sheltered contradictory desires that only destiny was capable of controlling.

However, we had something in common: the taste to live far from the mental toxins as hate and the jealousy that poison the existence of humans. I also knew that in this vast ring that is life, the fight wouldn't be easy. Soon, we would be confronted with our own problems, which we're going to solve somehow. Life, being unforeseeable, can go beyond one's own understanding of things.

Once again, day to day, I became aware of the extent of my misfortune. I was five years old when my mother died. My father had tried everything so that my mother's absence didn't affect my existence. But between times, I learned that it was normal to suffer, to feel bad, and to express it. I shut it in forever in a corner of my head, but yet the situation constantly haunted my memory. The first years of my life were martyrdom without end. During this tumultuous and violent period, I was plagued by a lack of confidence.

The difficulty to express and the endless solitude have darkened my soul. I underwent all sorts of odious treatments in spite of my father's warm affection, which was not sufficient to fill my mother's place. Now that I became an adult, I tried to understand the reasons of the sufferings that punctuated my daily life. I lived under a shell made of pain, anguish, and distress. I wanted this nightmare halted; then I interrogated God: "Why, Lord, why me?"

No one can answer this question. In search of comfort, of love, of tenderness, I confided myself to people who abandoned me before my miseries, vowed to a fate little enviable. The same sadness that came with me in my teenage years seemed to catch up with me to the first days of my adult life. While my mates were welcomed in their families like small princes, for my part, I passed sleepless nights to think about my mother; their indifference to me was very scornful. I felt decreased, humiliated, and rejected by my stepmother, who saw me not as a son but as a conqueror. My father locked himself in his hut for a whole day.

He was quiet and sad because he hated to see my stepmother making me suffer her scenes of unfounded and badly placed jealousy.

Fortunately, I could put to profit what I learned during my thirty days of initiation. I learned to know me, to resign me, and to resist. I cried without crying, and I laughed without laughing. It all came to reinforce my soul.

I knew that in this family in which I grew facing a resistant gate, my place was not there anymore, it was only elsewhere that I could find it. This reflection pushed me to exile myself far from my family that I liked so much. On my way to exile, I took a truck of public transportation from Sareboido to Koundara. While making our farewell in the big crowd of the market, Niang Mariam, with her tears, was miserable to see, and I had difficulty keeping mine.

"You are going to come back soon, my love, promise it."

"Yes, love, I promise it."

I waited for the departure crouched down in top of the truck, when I saw coming up in the same truck the most beautiful girl that I had ever seen. I prayed that she would not come to sit down close to me. Yet she came. We started a conversation. She was called Aissatou, and in ten minutes I was in love with her. She was seventeen years old and appeared fifteen. She had a perfect body, hot and shiny skin; silk hair, stiff and mad, that fell behind her; and a large and cool smile. What hurt to admit finally, she seemed to be interested a lot in me. To give myself courage, I told myself that after all, I had pleased a lot of women before Aissatou; but I had to also admit that all these women had been plain, except my girlfriend, Niang Mariam, who I loved so much. They were brave girls, with two legs, two breasts, two eyes, and everything that is necessary but without anything of particular moving in their aspect or in their subjects. This time it was quite the contrary. I could not stop my heart from beating more quickly as it did for

Niang Mariam. Aissatou had this heedless and cheerful beauty that one only sees in the very rich people. Every second with her possessed a surprising intensity. I lost my head. I realized with a painful lucidity that I lived one privileged moment of my life.

Similar splendor would never spend within reach of my head again. I knew it; I knew it as if I had read it.

Would I have the courage and intelligence to behave as I should? Would I be cool enough not to be terrorized by the possibility of blundering, not drive me more if I made one, to laugh at myself, to remain myself? I didn't want to play a role and yet, such an actor of one evening. Would I be capable, in this unique circumstance, to defeat this masochistic demon which paralyzes us and changes us into a jumping frog when happiness, without warning, touches us lightly on the cheek?

The time was magnificent, and the sun cooked us as surely as if we had been immobile. At the end of twenty minutes, the truck moved toward Koundara, raising such a reddish dust storm that upon arrival we all looked disguised. I had often met Aissatou thereafter. Some would say that I had conquered her; I would say rather I was conquered. After all I found a place to stay with a friend of my father's in Koundara

Before seeing her the second time again, I had succeeded in persuading myself that she was not so special as any other girl, that her shit didn't smell like roses, and that to lose her would have no big importance because Niang Mariam, my girlfriend of the village, always occupied more than half of my heart. I was very convinced that I succeeded in being perfectly natural, to defeat my demon, and to taste my reward. I tried to conquer her family's affection but I came up against her father's shy opposition, which went from smiling indifference to the most deliberate bad will. Aissatou and I passed the long hour sitting behind the fence that surrounded his family. Over us was the flank of the famous Mount Badiar. Koundara, the night, this city took airs of magic. So beautiful and so animated in the middle of the immense fields of rice in harvest, clearing an appetizing perfume, gleaming under the blue paleness of the moon, one always waited for the surprise of her father Mody Moundjirou, known for his lack of indulgence, taut and rigorous.

One evening that looked beautiful and restful, I embarked in the company of some girls with my friend Alpha Mahmoud Barry, known as Briams, an agronomic engineer who came from Conakry for a mission of long length in Koundara. Briams was not the uncommunicative kind, but he was a soccer fanatic. He often went to the stadium just to look at the performances of our common friend, Abdel Kader Kaba, who he admired so much, even though he played against the team of Mamou, Briams's native region. To the level of his agronomist's profession, Briams was very active but he always found moments to have fun with us. He liked to play the man of good living to seduce the girls so much that all beautiful girls circulated around him.

That day we amused ourselves so long that I surrendered late and exhausted at Aissatou's. "Then, my angel, you must really get bored here!" She made me notice while immediately giving me a hot kiss on the cheek. And we kissed like teenagers in quest of stronger sensations. But that day, Aissatou found something abnormal in my behavior.

"Say," she said, "I have the impression that you are not concentrated too much today. Your caresses are approximate and furthermore, I don't feel the virility of your arms too much. Are you sick?"

This question coming from Aissatou pained me a lot. But what to tell her? This last time, in fact, I became too timorous. Maybe I arrived at a stage of blockage! In any case, when it was time to climb the hill, curiously, all my strength left me, and Aissatou only had her eyes to cry. Neither did I want to go to consultation in the regional hospital because with these graduate physicians, thanks to their revolutionary productivity rather than to their medical assimilation, the risk was not the least.

"It is maybe due to fatigue. I worked a lot for my guardian these last weeks," I lied.

"And do you believe that such an argument is strong? Tell me what work you do to be exhausted also!!!"

Somewhere, Aissatou was right, because in my new function, my guardian assigned me to supervise his workers in his fields of rice; my task limited itself to sit and to watch. Beyond that, I shouted to the workers who, yet, produced the biggest part of the activities operating my guardian's agricultural enterprise. And to say that, for all this work, their salary hardly passed guaranteed minimum wage, there was what being reasonable!

They looked at me, wordlessly, to say, with their red eyes. Don't believe that Aissatou, while asking me such a question, was jealous of me! Well, on the contrary, what interested her was my purse. Anyway, to this level, she had never been disappointed in me. But only she didn't want that I am the biggest loser in the current phase.

After a last attempt to get over the hill, and another failure, she found that it was better that I go to the hospital. When I went there, the physician recommended me an absolute rest for one week. Aissatou could not support this length and would come to my house every night to stay with me until late. Her father hit her and forbid her to see me. Learning it, I immersed myself in a big depression; I didn't eat and didn't sleep anymore. Without knowing why, at the same moment, some advice from Byllon crossed my mind. He said this, more or less: "Know that in life, everything has its time."

He had told it to us during the nocturnal vigils of our circumcision. After my medical rest, I went with Aissatou to see my friend, Briams, to ask for his opinion on my case; He says to me "don't you worry, this girl is for you no matter what"; I offered him a box of Milo cigarettes, his favorite. Although he took it, he told me that three weeks ago, he decided not to smoke anymore. And since this day until he left Koundara, I didn't see him with a cigarette again. This feature of character, even though he didn't make me any effect in the immediate, began to make interrogate me on my behavior of the moment.

One week later, Aissatou's father, Mody Moundjirou asked to see me at their residence. Upon my arrival, her father welcomed me timidly, as if he had not asked me to come. He told me, "Listen to me, boy, my daughter only cries and won't eat because of you. I warn you, if something happens to her, your days will be over. Do I make myself clear?"

"Yes, father," I answered.

Some minutes after, all alone in the house, I met face to face with Aissatou, who threw herself into my arms. We were all happy. From time to time, when our eyes locked, I felt a special sensation cross my heart. Was I liking her or did I want her, or was this a simple admiration for her? Me, Nouhou, to be liking a girl who was not Niang Mariam, the first love of my life? I had never imagined such a distress in my sentimental life, of where my incredulity as for having such a feeling for someone else other than Niang Mariam!

I looked at Aissatou to speak to me. Her oratory and her intelligence didn't allow me to be indifferent. In the end, she got me to agree to a date at the regional movie theater, which was showing a popular Indian movie, and as she didn't want to feel alone, she asked my presence.

Being new in Koundara City, the movie theater was a place that I had only seen from the outside.

And I wasn't an urban type person. I found it too influential . But by love, I accepted Aissatou's invitation.

That Saturday, I would finally see the inside of this movie theater, which looked above all like a merchandise storage, and I made the acquaintance of a few youngsters of my age, such as Moussa Diawo, Sow Hawa, Sow Waranka, Mama Diaboula, Dabo Mariam, Aissatou Dow, Bah Hawa, Pascal Nioké, and Dany, to mention these only.

"Look, Nouhou," Aissatou said, "I introduced you to all these young people in manner of friendship to allow you to climb with endurance the highest walks of Venus."

I confessed straightaway that I had no understanding of what she was saying. I knew that Venus was the Roman goddess of love, but as for these high walks to climb, I got lost a little bit.

Once back home, I thought about what I had to offer to Aissatou in return.

Was it also necessary that is a gift of the same nature?

Two days later in the evening, back from work, I passed Aissatou's house; I found her helping her mother to cook dinner. "Aissatou, good evening!" I said. "I do hope that I don't disturb you."

"You are welcome. Can I bring you water to drink?"

"No, thank you."

The whole time that our talk lasted, my thoughts only went to the gesture that I had to make her on my turn. Did she wait indeed for something of me?

What is this that I was able to bring to her and that she didn't have, her the daughter of one of the biggest tradesman of the city of Koundara?

I recognized my big weakness for the woman, but on the other hand I took the gifts that others offered to me very seriously. And on that plan, Aissatou admired me a lot.

"What would you make of it if I invited you one day to Madina Badiar, my native village?" I asked Aissatou.

"I don't see an inconvenience in that."

I left Aissatou without forgetting to hand her an envelope containing five hundred Guinean sylis, the national currency that I had taken care to close well.

In any case, she had shown no hostile reaction at first sight. Having let me before the portal of her house, she wished me a good night.

It had been eight months since I had made the acquaintance of Aissatou. Reciprocally, we hadn't stopped seeing each other. She hadn't said anything about my gesture as to whether she liked it or not. But always it was the same ambiance that reigned between us. I had not finished asking these questions when a visitor appeared at my house. I told a small boy to go and open the door. Some moments later, he came back with a big cardboard box of gifts that he deposited before me.

"Brother Nouhou! It is the girl that tells me to give you this cardboard."

"And herself? Where did she pass?"

"She put me in charge of telling you that she had a setback."

I opened the cardboard and I discovered with surprise three pants and three beautiful shirts, tailored to my exact measure, with a word from Aissatou.

"It is not possible! What Aissatou wants from me?"

When I saw her, I thanked her orally but she acted as if it was nothing. She told me that she wanted to buy me a beautiful pair of shoes but she changed her mind because she told me that in Africa, it is said (even proven) that if you buy a pair of shoes for your boyfriend, he will walk away wearing the same shoes, to leave you forever!

What was curious, was that the total cost of these clothes was distinctly superior to the amount of five hundreds sylis that I had given her in the closed envelope!

One year passed, and I began to look at Aissatou another way. There were moments where she slept at my house, but always refused to let me undress her. She told me that I was too hurried, and that love was not a short race.

"Know that my first totem, it is to share my man with another woman," she had warned me one day when she asked that we take our relationship more seriously. "I cannot make you a promise, but it is a question of time she said

Another time, she required me to have a physical checkup in the hospital. When it was done and she saw that I was in good health, I shouted victory without knowing what she thought of me internally.

That day, I wanted to give her a few soft kisses, but she averted her lips, warning me that she would break definitely with me. I had been patient long enough. I ignored all girls who circulated around me, to abstain of all without making her bend completely.

To dissuade the girls who circulated around me, I told them that I had a very jealous girlfriend who was capable of piercing their eyes. From then on, Aissatou became my only companion.

We went together to the stadium to see my best friend Abdel Kader Kaba, who was a real star, play soccer with all his talent, and everywhere our intimacy was well able to bring us closer.

At times, Aissatou had an attitude with me. Yet I did everything in my power to satisfy her, but in vain.

"Aissatou, tell me what I did to you to be angry at me? I gave you an envelope that you returned me. I made my physical checkup, broke with all these girls who circulated around me, just to show you that I like you."

"Me, you like me?"

"I like you, Aissatou. It is true, with you, I feel so strong … "

Was Aissatou therefore not sure of my love for her? Or was she studying me?

I was very close to discouragement, to depression, when a sudden idea came to me. I remembered that often, during some of our talks, Aissatou told me to like nature. Was it necessary to bring her something close to it? I didn't estimate the range of a flower more for the heart of an African woman. Once I attempted it and I was terribly disappointed, because the one I offered the flower threw it savagely in my face, making me believe that it was an insane thing and that only money counted for her. But one didn't say that "Who doesn't risk nothing has anything?"

I took the resolution therefore to go to a florist to buy a pretty bouquet of pink flowers, so this time, if the result was negative, then I would decide to break forever with Aissatou.

When I arrived at Aissatou's house in the evening, at the door, my heart beat. She came to open it, a large smile on her face, and when I offered her my bouquet of flowers, she hugged me very hard, as I would never have imagined it my life. It was in the vicinity of midnight when our true romance began. For the first time, I had to lovingly grind the lips of Aissatou, and under the effects of the rose-bruise colors of the night-light of her room, that gave a special seal to this moment , she asked me sweetly, "Don't you want to be my spouse? I now realize that you truly like me. It is necessary that I speak of it tomorrow to my mother."

"Why?" I asked.

"I would simply like that she is the first person to be informed."

"Don't forget that your father is fundamentally against our friendship."

"My mother and I will make him change opinion because it is my mother who is always harassing me to get married."

Aissatou put her hand on mine while advancing her cool breath. I kissed her. I pulled her to me. We were wild about each other.

Her father, noting the strength of our deep love, had been afraid that his daughter would get pregnant out of wedlock; he hastened to make her get married to an old man, who could be her grandfather. Aissatou died one year later while delivering her first child.

When my father had learned that I had left, he got angry with my mother-in-law and left to find me.

When he found me with the family of one of his friends in Koundara the regional capital, he tried to convince me to return to the family, but his friend defended my decision to leave because above all, I was traditionally an adult and capable of making my own decisions.

At twilight evening that seemed yet serene to him, my father, surprised and shocked, decided to find me, which cost him thirty miles of nocturnal walking before reaching Koundara, the regional capital where I had taken shelter.

When he arrived at four o'clock in the morning under a thick brunette, my father seemed exhausted by the physical effort and by the sadness that gnawed him mercilessly. That day, I was awake at dawn. My father and his friend at whose home I took refuge were already present in the antechamber.

An unknown man and my landlord's wife came to look for me in my room to take me out the small door. We went outside. In the run illuminated by the pale gleam of dawn, one heard the concert of the roosters that, from the tenor to the bass while passing by the baritone, tried to take their spectators out of the arms of Morpheme.

Suddenly, my landlord's wife challenged me in these terms: "Listen, young man, do you realize what you have put your father through? We are here to help you to not commit the mistakes that can be costly to you. We're going to bring you back in the antechamber where your father is but know in advance that you must never contradict him."

In the antechamber, the unknown man motioned me to a stool, on which I sat down, and he addressed me in these terms: "We, your elders, advise you to return to the village to continue to live and to learn the Quran with your venerated father because God didn't give luck to all children to have such a father."

This advice created a feeling of sadness in me; I told myself internally that to remain far from my family was the only right thing for me, while not necessarily for another, and better still, life is as we discern it.

I continued to search this antechamber for a person who could understand my pain and sustain me in my position.

Suddenly, a vivid smile formed on the lips of my father's friend, whose big shiny eyes seemed to wave to me that he had just seized the expression of my sad face. My father's mysterious silence, which sharpened my curiosity, didn't leave me any other alternative than to struggle against my own heart, which consumed itself with grief. I had to ask my heart to be quiet; it didn't obey me, and headstrong like a slipper , it played me the incredible turn.

My heart started beating so fast that I lost control of my movements. I quite confided in God, the all powerful, because whatever happens to you, life is always beautiful and is worth living.

When my father's friend asked me if I agreed to return to the village with my father, I answered politely that I wished to remain in Koundara indeed and to look for work. Immediately, my father seized a trinket made of china and smashed it before me while raging with anger. No one dared to contradict him. I didn't have another recourse than that of despair because I had never seen my father in such an state of anger.

Then his friend told him, "Listen, Thierno Demba, your son has just passed to the adult age, let him learn to live his own life. If you sowed the seed, don't prevent it from growing and blooming. Thierno Demba," said his friend, "things changed, our children don't want us to tell them what to do. They refuse everything that we give to them. They want to find elsewhere what is really only at home. What to do? Must we make our children our adversaries? No! I don't think so. Life, early or late, will teach them the truth."

As soon as he finished speaking, my father cleared his throat and said to his friend, "It is true, everything that you have said is just. We are in a world that we don't know. Today, there is not anything more, not of ties between father and son, no more loyalty between friends, no more of consideration between young and old. However, I wanted to make of this child a big scholar of Islam to follow the traces of his ancestors."

"I thought that was it," exclaimed his friend, "because I know your loyalty is toward Islam; however, to want to force the situation is not going to help, Thierno Demba."

My father appeared pensive. He raised his eyes to the ceiling, then turned to look toward me and examined me head to toe and then smiled; then he pronounced these prophetic words and said, "And you too, my son, one day life will teach you the truth."

On the following day, my father had to return to the village. At his departure, he asked me to come with him halfway. We began to speak of the long road joining Koundara and Madina Badiar, with the howling strips of dust wind that ravaged all on their paths. I prayed him without respite to borrow the passenger's truck.

He merely told me, "Ha, my son, when I was your age I didn't care about a truck; alas, the things changed so quickly. Today, the young don't have ardor."

I remained, mouth agape.

"Dad, you will be exhausted too much, borrow the truck," I suggested again.

"You tell histories," he said. "Me, I am poor and old but active," he added. "Believe me, my son," he continued, "to walk on foot will do me a lot of good."

Was this the reason that he often asked us to massage his feet?

I smiled while admiring him from his feet to the head, him that was my father, my mother, and my Master of Quran. I told myself internally that he was right, laziness doesn't know how to take itself of it that to the weak.

"Thank you, God, I am again in good health," he said while surprising me to measure the extent of this long road that he had to travel all alone.

Suddenly, my father appeared pensive to my eyes; his quiet look was full of mysteries. I kept carefully away from any subversive subject and anything that might appear to be disobedience. However, I felt very sad that he had to separate with me for the first time since my birth fifteen years ago.

"My son," he said, "do you realize how much I am pained?"

"Yes, Dad, I understand your pain, but take courage like all other fathers who separate with their children. It is certainly not easy but it is not the same as death, just a temporary separation. Let me learn to search so that one day I can come to your help," I suggested.

"Okay, my son, know that you don't live anymore with your parents but with others. Be polite, honest, and discreet. As for the five prayers per day, I recommend them to you more than all. The respect of these recommendations will lead you infallibly to success." He passed me the Holy Quran and told me, "It's your companion and your protector; you must be faithful to it."

I advanced toward my father, and he opened his arms to me in a redeeming gesture of infinite tenderness. Suddenly, a light beating of the heart attacked me. It was the paternal love that devoured my adolescence.

It was downwind, and the howling dust that arrived at the top of Mount Badiar and that collapsed in passionate waves on the trees stunted on the inside, and on this miserable and craggy track, which I always remember, I saw my father moving away gradually as if getting lost in a dust cloud. I should have stopped myself one instant while my heart blamed me for having resisted my father's paternal desires. But it was necessary and unavoidable. I took the path then back to the city while looking back at my poor father, who I had just sent back with mercy. The wind sometimes screamed and hissed strong so that I asked myself how my father was going to make it. From time to time, an even more vicious gust than the others seemed to rob me of all strength.

On my path, I decided to pass by the village of Kamabi before returning to Koundara. On the road, some goats strolled on a discolored earth, craggy and gray. We were in Sarakollé country, in the region of Koundara, an arid soil where nothing seemed to grow. In this village of the thin melts of the Mount Badiar, an old man splices in his barrow, with slow gestures, the batteries of humid bricks to make them dry in the sun. They will serve for the construction of the new clinic . Some laughing girls discussed around   the boundary mark fountain; they invited me to cool myself in their home. I accept voluntarily and went inside a house, where the explosion of color contrasted with the surrounding moonscape. I visited then all the dwellings of Kamabi, noting that none were similar to another. The village, with walls of ocher-gray earth, contrasted with the insides with iridescent colors that danced on the walls. One finds abstract geometric shapes drawn there with care, irregular, or mosaics of quick colors overlapped with ingenuity, or others that spread the blue complexion from the soil sky to the ceiling, in a damaged magic.. In this semi-desert region, the culture of the rice once lived, with rarefied water, and savage animals, previously so frequent in this region of big hunters, now disappeared. But the men didn't wait to see their decline. Since several generations, they left to look for what provided for their family's needs. First to Senegal as seasonal workers in the peanut plantations, then in Sefadu (Republic of Sierra Leone). The separations became longer and the returns to the country, uncertain. Then the women, meeting alone a good part of the year, decorated their houses themselves while developing this fantastic art wall, named Meltal. Back in the village, the men answered merely, when one evoked the talent of their wives, that it is a business of women!

Here is how they indeed obtained the indispensable materials for the Meltal. The white was achieved from a chalky stone, soaked a whole night in water, dried, sifted, and mixed with flour or gumbo to adhere to the wall. The ocher color is from an earth that they find about ten kilometers from the village. And the red clay was earth mixed with the dung of cow or the fruit of the djebe. It also served to return the black and brilliant soils.

In some houses, the walls make a display of big white tiles, blacks and ocher to the regular features; elsewhere, some zigzags run on the whole length of the wall. Finally, about every five years, the women repaint their house to fill the boredom, and also to give pleasure to their husbands upon their return. With time, each man wants his house to be the most beautiful. The family's women come to help with the decoration. The preparation of the paint—to crush, to mix, and to macerate the different products and the research of the basic materials—can take one month.

As for the painting of a slot, it can take one to three weeks according to the drawn motives . Its finish gives the opportunity to make a feast!

Today, the women decorate the shelves with teapots and plates of Chinese decor, and hang on the walls the prayer-rugs coming from Mecca, spangled sandals, and photos of the absent men. All their goods pass in the decoration of the house. The Chinese plates and the dishes will serve later for their daughters. While waiting, the mothers expose all their wealth.

Thanks to resources sent by the emigrants, the big borough became a real oasis of peace, with one administrative precinct, and already it has its mosque, its schools, and its clinic under construction, without counting the forges. The joy of living of these women is so active, full of creativeness and passion, the region of Koundara breathes a real well-being that one leaves with regret.

However, Koundara is a strange and extremely hot city; the only way to survive there is to pretend that the heat doesn't exist. One accepts the heat while trying not to think that there are regions of the globe where, at the same moment, others freezes from their toes to their heads. What does we can against the law of nature?

That night, in my nocturnal thought, I reviewed my village corner after corner as if I was there indeed. I knew that this new world that had attracted me sat full of obstacles and full of mysteries. While in my village, all was easy for me. There was not a fight or a banditry; everybody liked each other and helped each other.

However, I was determined not to let any respite to my main enemies, which were fear and laziness; these two looked for me without success, as if one looked for the mouse in the cat's house.

It was indeed destiny that made me a call and that had paved me a long path to browse. On this path, happiness and success waited for me. Thanks to destiny and to my father's blessing, I succeeded in taking care of the whole family without taking into account the past. I invited my stepmother's only son to come to share my happiness under my own roof for ten successful years. My stepmother regretted all her acts and behaved henceforth like a true mom while knowing that my moral injuries, of which she was the author, were going to leave their mark for the rest of my life.

During my thirty days of initiation, I learned that a man must not move back from the difficulties of life and that by dint of looking for, one always ended up finding. This traditional African oral value revealed the advent of a new era of my adult life. My moral and material difficulties yielded to prosperity, and life, which was previously for me a mixture of sadness, absurdity, and hope, had become again all joy and laughter. My human qualities to which I'm always prideful helped me not to have feelings of vengeance. All happened before God, and only he is capable to judge the facts and the acts accomplished by men.

Speaking of the circumcision, the term designates the ablation of a part of the sexual organ, so much masculine than feminine, whatever is the size of this ablation.

In the Hebrew language, the term *milah*—which means "cut"—designates the masculine circumcision. The former will use the expression *berit milah*—"the alliance of the cut"—to dedicate the agreement that Yahveh concluded with Abraham.

In return for the obligation to circumcise all members of his community, he promised him the supremacy on his progeny: "To you and to your race after you, I will give the country where you will stay, the whole country of Canaan, in perpetuity in possession, and I will be your God." (Genesis 17:8) It is by this alliance that the Bible distinguishes the Jews from the non-Jews, these last being qualified by the pejorative term of uncircumcised.

In the Arabian culture, the act of the circumcision, masculine and feminine, got along like a conditional to marriage. He is designated by the term *Khatana*, which indicates the marking of a seal. To this subject, a Muslim scholar of the fourteenth century explained: "No one denies that the amputation of this skin is a designation of servitude."

The obligatory character of the masculine circumcision of the Jews and the mutilation that Abraham imposed on his sons and his tribe's men ensues directly at the Muslim. In Judaism, the milah is worth all other commands, and the Jews give the priority to the circumcision on the eighth day in the respect of the Sabbath or a parent's funeral. The uncircumcised are considered like impure; the Jewish norms forbid to socialize with them, to eat their food, or to give them a woman in marriage. Although the Quran doesn't make explicit mention of circumcision, it is considered obligatory in reference to the Sunnah—or tradition—of Mohammed, the second source of the Muslim right. For some modern authors, it is placed at the head of the laws of nature enacted by God to the believers or to the converts. In Islam, the defenders of masculine circumcision consider those that deny its obligatory character as apostates deserving capital punishment.

As for feminine circumcision, it is considered by her masculine promoters like a deserving act and purifier for the woman because, as one of them expresses it, "She keeps it of the leanings that excessively excite her sexual instinct."

The reasons for circumcision vary according to religions, communities, and so on. Every social group advances its own reasons. But the truth is that the medical, traditional circumcision, or Anglo-Saxon fashion phenomenon, doesn't rest on any justification except the one of Abraham, and makes itself without the agreement of the children.

Several groups worry understandably of the excision of the small girls in the setting of sexual mutilations. It is very likely that in some years, these same groups will fight for the small boys against a retrograde practice. The babies have, as the women and the adult men, the right to have their bodies. Who can bring only one rational argument in favor of this practice? Who can sustain that a child cannot have his body freely?

The circumcision is a nontherapeutic intervention, that means that it is not necessary in one point of medical view. The parents who decide to circumcise their newborns often make it for religious, social, or cultural reasons. They should possess information about its risks and advantages. In any case, it is useful to debate with your baby's physician. The risks of medical circumcision are rare. Although serious complications are also rare, they exist, however. The newborn's circumcision is associated with such surgical mistakes as the extraction of too big a surface of skin. In rare cases, the methods and the medication to relive the pain can cause side effects and complications. For the case of advantages of circumcision, some may say that it slightly decreases the risk of cancer of the penis later in life. However, this type of cancer is of an extreme rarity.

According to recent American medical studies on circumcision, it shows that circumcision removes the most sensitive parts of the penis. A sensitivity study of the adult penis in circumcised and uncircumcised men shows that the uncircumcised penis is significantly more sensitive. The most sensitive location on the circumcised penis is the circumcision scar on the ventral surface. Five locations on the uncircumcised penis that are routinely removed at circumcision are significantly more sensitive than the most sensitive location on the circumcised penis.

In addition, the glands (head) of the circumcised penis is less sensitive to fine touch than the glands of the uncircumcised penis. The tip of the foreskin is the most sensitive region of the uncircumcised penis, and it is significantly more sensitive than the most sensitive area of the circumcised penis.

This study presents the first extensive testing of fine touch pressure thresholds of the adult penis. The monofilament testing instruments are calibrated and have been used to test female genital sensitivity.

Male circumcision affects female sexual enjoyment. A survey of women who have had sexual experience with circumcised and anatomically complete partners showed that the anatomically complete penis was preferred over the circumcised penis. Without the foreskin to provide a movable sleeve of skin, intercourse with a circumcised penis resulted in female discomfort: increased friction, abrasion, and loss of natural secretions. Respondents overwhelmingly concurred that the mechanics of coitus were different for the two groups of men. Unaltered men tended to thrust more gently with shorter strokes.

A study published in *The Journal of the American Medical Association* found that circumcision provided no significant prophylactic benefit and that circumcised men were more likely to engage in various sexual practices. Specifically, circumcised men were significantly more likely to masturbate and to participate in heterosexual oral sex than uncircumcised men.

In the Republic of Zambia, the ritual of the *makishi* takes place at the end of the *mukanda*, a ritual of initiation for boy aged eight to twelve years. This ritual is celebrated by the Vaka Chiyamaq Cha Mukwamayi communities, to which belong the Luvale people, Chokwes, Luchazis, and Mbundas, established in the provinces northwest and west of Zambia.

It is usually in the beginning of the dry season that the young boys leave their home to live during one to three months in a camp in full savanna, far from their village. This separation of the boys from the outside world marks their symbolic death as children. During their retirement in the camp, the insiders are called *Tundanji*, those that don't belong to the world of the living. The mukanda consists of the circumcision of the insiders, tests of courage, and lessons on their future role of men and husbands. Every insider sees himself assigned a masked character, who comes along with his initiation. These characters include the Chisaluke, which represents a rich and powerful man, strong with a big spiritual influence, notably; the Mupala, the "Lord" of the mukanda and protective mind endowed with supernatural faculties; the Pwevo, feminine character representing the ideal woman, charged of the musical accompaniment of the rituals and the dances; and the Makishi, which evokes the mind of a deceased ancestor come back in the world of the living to help the boys.

The end of the mukanda is marked by a ceremony of recognition named *chilende*. The whole village assembles to watch the Makishi to dance and entertain the public with their pantomimes, until the new insiders leave the camp and are restored like adults in their communities and their families. This ritual has an educational function insofar as it permits the transmission of survival and knowledge of nature, sexuality, religious beliefs, and the social values of the community.

The mukanda, which once lasted several months, has been reduced to one month to adapt to the school calendar. It comes up against a strong opposition from the Christian churches. Socioeconomic changes have also deprived it of its spiritual and sacred dimension. A lot of adult men, supposed to transmit the tradition, leave their village for the city, in search of a better livelihood. The benefits of the makishi are also distorted by the fact that they are reduced to the rank of simple entertainment for the social gatherings, the meetings of political parties, and the tourists, thanks to the customs and to the African tradition.

To consider the African culture like a very out-of-date and helpless historic phenomenon is to see the cultural and scientific future quite upside-down.

Throughout her culture, Africa has non-negotiable values that suffered from a lack of consideration characterized by the race to politics that generate both moral and material profits.

Contrary to masculine circumcision, the excision of girls is a barbaric ritual and source of a lot of suffering. They are immobilized by strong arms on the soil just next to a hole of some centimeters dug for the circumstance; it takes place without anesthesia and without a minimum of hygiene, using a knife that dates of several decades, very often covered with rust. Some small girls die by loss of a lot of blood the very day of their excision or some weeks after.

A hundred and twenty million women in the world underwent sexual mutilations, of which more than a hundred million were in Africa, according to the World Health Organization (WHO). The WHO and feminine associations fight to eradicate these cultural practices, whose nonreligious origin gets lost in the night of the times, and which are very painful to live for those that are victims of it. These genital mutilations, current in several countries of the world, whose goal is to attenuate the woman's sexual desire to preserve her virginity before the marriage and to insure then her fidelity, obey different customs. The excision, which consists in the ablation of the clitoris, represents about 80 percent of the mutilations in West Africa. The infibulations that add in more the partial ablation of the lips of the feminine sex is applied in many other African countries. These interventions are done on newborns, on little girls, or on teenagers without anesthesia and often in bad conditions of hygiene with knives, razor blades, or even pieces of non-sterilized glass. They drag deadly risks of hemorrhage and infections and later, by choice, sterility and pregnancy problems, such as difficult childbirths and many deaths of the mother or the child. Undermining the integrity of the woman's body, they also have heavy psychological aftermaths, from frigidity to anxiety, while passing by unrests of behavior. Why then the virginity? It is the leitmotif of the supporters of the cult of the hymen! It essentially rests on the bleeding of this membrane at the time of the wedding night. A bleeding that, in the custom practiced in some African countries and elsewhere in the world, is judicious to symbolize the newlywed's purity. Yet, the hymen doesn't always bleed at the time of the first penetration.

Under the ascendancy of a culture that makes virginity a requirement and that concentrates the honor of a whole family on this "tip of membrane," some women face a painful dilemma either because they succumbed to the pleasures of the flesh or because they were victims of a sexual aggression (a trauma to which they don't wish to add a domestic drama). To such a point that some have only an obsession: to bleed the day of the marriage.

And all is good to get some drops of hemoglobin on the immaculate sheets of the nuptial bed and the screams of joy of the matrons. Some opt for traditional methods, and some resort to the big means: the hymenoplastie or reconstruction of the hymen.

Exorbitant and in doubtful and dangerous conditions of hygiene. Of the critiques that reinforce the population who estimate that the virginity is not absolute. For them, to be virgin is not still a quality. It is the case in the Democratic Republic of Congo. In some regions of this country, sexual experience is rather considered like a virtue, and the excessive sexual desire of the women is not a crime.

These different stances demonstrate well that the virginity makes debate. A debate to which the writing of Afrik decided to contribute while inviting you to penetrate this universe of true false virgins, to understand their incentives in the setting of a file dedicated to this question. .

Thanks to the constant pressure of the World Health Organization, to the awareness of the women, at a time victims and organizers of these punishments, that this practice, the most often secret, begin to move back.

However, the African governments should show evidence of firmness while knowing that they have the duty to bring the believers to abandon this practice by a sustained education program based on the spiritual principles and strong scientific information.

It's an opportunity for me to return a vibrant homage to the African oral tradition, the real cradle of the universal culture that always transmits itself from father to son. If the West has a culture of integrated development, Africa has a social culture based on the oral character in spite of some systematized test up to here hardly encouraged and badly cared for; because the Africans always tend to believe that to educate themselves, only the Western culture must be taken into consideration. It's the result of a real brain-washing initiated by the ancestors of colonization that means to create and to maintain a versatile politic of dependency in the former colonies so that their people stagnate under their eternal domination.

Instead of promoting the development of the culture, our governments practice the politics of tense hands to receive debts for development projects that are never achieved. These debts, which no state is able to repay, are annulled from time to time under very coercive conditions by the clubs of Paris, London, and Rome.

Better again, since the eternal silence fell on the famous and intelligible voices such as Senghor, of Camara Laye, of Cheikh Anta Diop, of Hampaté Bâ, and so on, the African culture sank itself more and more in an astonishing oubliette. The governments and the African men of culture are the only ones capable to act to save what's salvageable. One doesn't perpetuate anything but to save one's own culture to avoid killing oneself in the future. The past prepares the future, but if one doesn't have any inheritance and waits from day to day for the present, one is cut off the future.

In short, Africa is a continent of diverse peoples and civilizations as heterogeneous as the Peulh, the Yoruba, and the Mandingos to the west and the Swahilis and the Bantu in the East. Hasty foreign observers only see a mosaic of African tribes without obvious ties, which the vagaries of migrations and colonial strategies forced to live together. These peoples, certainly different by their origins and by their languages, have learned , centuries after centuries, to share the African vital space, to operate a complex human mixture, and to ascertain between them indisputable psychological, historic, and cultural complicities.

It's well more than the double notions of ethnology and anthropology that pretend to know this African Earth where the multiple contrasts always reflected themselves, as by a game of optics, on a tough bottom of unity and consistency in spite of some rare cases of political and social turbulence.

Previously, the oral tradition held a non-negligible place in the process of diffusion of the culture. With the real advent of the book and the use of reading in the current sense of the term, which dates to the beginning of the colonial era with the first missionaries and the apparition of the first colonial schools, the oral tradition lost its place.

In modern societies, the book remains the privileged means of diffusion of the culture, in spite of the fantastic development of the audiovisual diffusion means, television and the Internet, that seem to want more and more to supplant it in a definitive way.

The development of the book in a country is a function of the reading needs of the populations and vice versa. The needs of reading are motivated, stimulated, and maintained by abundance and the quality of the available literature.

In oral civilizations, speech is the man, from where the deep respect of the traditional narrations bequeathed by the past, of which is permitted to embellish the shape or the poetic turn. But the branch remains unchangeable through the centuries, transported by a stupendous memory that's a characteristic of oral tradition peoples.

In modern civilization, paper substituted itself for speech. It's he that hires the man. But can one say in all certainty, in these conditions, that the written source is worthier of confidence than the oral source, constantly controlled by the traditional environment?

With rare exceptions, the oral character is the common denominator of the cultural foundation. In African society, speech is more than a prosaic tool of communication or awarding; it's not even the appendage of the humans; previous to these, she exists by herself, for herself.

A vehicle of knowledge and wisdom, speech is also the venom that kills the enemy, the spark that triggers the thunderbolt, the spell that bewitches the very beloved.

So the African peasant who deeply believes in the virtue of the words, of its force, of the efficiency of the speech, is able to maintain and to domesticate the occult strengths of the symbols, the rituals, and the magic formulas. These people that one qualifies, wrongfully, as illiterate are not as much deprived of culture. Their cultures are oral, often millennial, and include treasures of wisdom, of art to live. The people of black Africa didn't know from early on the use of writing, and during a long time this practice was reserved to a literate intellectual elite in Arabia. Therefore, our entire cultural heritage is again in the oral tradition. This is how the transmission of knowledge, religious teaching, initiation to myths, and the education of the children made themselves through oral speeches. Oral literature was always and remained again the ideal shape of expression in our countries where the majority of the population is illiterate and leads a communal life in the outdoors, thanks to the tradition that's a real method of life in community and life in family. It rests on a dynamic of rich and varied factors before being a proven source of deep knowledge of nature and humanity.

Previously, this knowledge transmitted itself regularly from generation to generation, by the rituals of initiation and by the different shapes of traditional education.

In my research, I understood that the African culture endures a disparagement that dates back to the colonial period.

During this historic time, the colonists made us believe that their culture was superior to ours. In school, one told us that our ancestors were Gallic. The language and the culture taught forcibly influenced our behavior and our way of thinking. Today one makes us believe that our continent is cursed, and immigration made us believe that we could only regress, we are already so low. Yet God has created the universe without borders so that all his creatures live there without constraint and in harmony, but by the strength of an egoism proper to the nature of these creatures in question, the universe becomes a place of antagonism to the contempt of the divine will.

All human community is governed by rules and principles founded on tradition, language, life-style, and thought, together with its genius and its own personality. However, the slavery and the colonization on the cultural plan, entailed the depersonalization of the black peoples of the world, falsifying their identity and their history, systematically disparaging and fighting their cultural values, encouraging the formation of an elite thus too often acculturated and acquired to the eternal assimilation.

It's important to me that the black peoples of the world become aware of entering finally into a common will to reinforce the understanding between them in order to answer their own aspirations and to strengthen a fraternity and a solidarity integrated within a vast cultural unit that transcends the divergences that the race of history imposed on them unjustly.

To reach these objectives, the rich and the intellectuals of the black world must play an efficient role as well in the cultural blossoming between the black peoples by an efficient political help with regard to the collective of creation that favors the individual creators. The black people of this world must recognize that it's important to establish cultural cooperation between them. There are factors of closeness and reciprocal enrichment of their cultures having to express itself under the shape of a double current of exchanges between all black peoples.

Also, it is important to make the black man more interested in culture and education, to get rid of this negative phenomenon that is about to make a black man a subordinate being. Part of it is about laziness to read. For example, in the subways in New York City, only two out of ten people who read books or newspapers, on their way home or to work, are black. Instead of reading, black men prefer to listen to music. It's often seen that on the way to school, black children have Walkman devices at their ears, absorbed by music rather than by their school duties. It's necessary without mistake to take a deepened awareness to fight against this negative phenomenon and face the realities to which black people are confronted.

Our youngsters must realize that expertise is one of the criteria that today determines access to a good paying job. However, expertise doesn't acquire itself without education, from which one can hope to acquire mastery and expertise.

One of the conditions to arrive there is to keep informed of all new developments of science and technology. Therefore, they must frequent libraries and read in order to be more educated and more informed.

The African continent was the birthplace of the *homininae* subfamily and the genus *Homo*, including eight species, of which only *Homo sapiens* survive. All the earliest *homininae* species have been found in Africa, and Africa alone, according to Richard Leakey, Kenyan anthropologist. The fossil trail of our origins begins in East Africa's Great Rift Valley, where upright-walking human ancestors appeared about 5 million years ago; modern humans also originated in Africa. The continent's tremendous range of habitats—from rain forests to savanna—favored early human evolution. Climate and vegetation changed over time. New conditions posed evolutionary challenges that led to greater species diversity and, eventually, to our ancestors. Human culture in Africa is as old as the human race, and includes Neolithic (10,000 BC) rock engravings, the glacial age petroglyphs (carvings or line drawings on rock, especially made by prehistoric people) of early hunter-gatherers in the dry grasslands of North Africa, the Nome's (A sort of Administrative division) of ancient Egypt.(BC3100)-

Africa is one continent with several worlds. The continent of Africa covers an area of around 30 million square kilometers, one-fifth of the landmass of the Earth, and has more than fifty countries. Its geographical features are diverse and range from tropical wet or rain forest, with rainfall of 250 to 380 centimeters, to tropical dry areas. Mount Kilimanjaro (height 5,895 meters) remains capped with snow all the year round, whereas the Sahara is the largest and hottest desert on the Earth. Africa has a diverse plant life ranging from scrub, savanna, desert shrub, and a variety of vegetation growing on mountains as well as in the tropical rain forest and deciduous forest.

Like nature, 800 million people of Africa have evolved a cultural milieu that is a study in contrast and has several dimensions.

The economic and social development of a country doesn't depend solely on capital and work, as the economists and the liberal tradition suggest. Culture is just as determining. In *The Society of Confidence*, which appeared in 1995, the French academician Alain Peyrefitte explained exactly that the big theories that placed economic resources (raw materials, funds, growth rate) in the center of the development passed, according to him, the factors of cultural order, which were relegated to the rank of "menus satellites," which had to be considered as the essential motor of progress.

Indeed, the intangible and immaterial elements of the culture condition mentalities. It's why they represent a real pedestal for the society . If one disregards them, if one doesn't situate them to the heart of the problem of development, they risk turning into insurmountable obstacles. Programmed on a big scale, culture could become an asset for the closeness of the black peoples of the North and the South separated by the race of history.

It rains the shortest path of a man to the other. By the mediation of the culture, some true exchanges can settle, some sincere and deep regards can weave themselves, in confidence, dignity and respect between the black people through the world .

Every black person whose ancestors are slaves by the strength of history, not by the nature of their birth, has a moral obligation to go back to his African roots to get rid of the division gate with its negative effects expressly trained to make of the black man an eternal subordinate. If there was not a reparation again in favor of blacks whose ancestors were slaves, it is because the black peoples remain divided again by culture, geography, and politics. All these obstacles are easily surmountable with will and determination. To stand up as one and to speak with one voice will ignite the sleeping power of black people.

It's necessary that black peoples preserve and develop their own personality while creating a common language sustained by a common alphabet to allow them to speak of themselves. From then on, they will be able to speak of their history to the other and not to the other, as scholars say, speak of the blacks to the blacks. To arrive at such an awareness, the black peoples as a whole must find a common cultural identity because they belong to the same origins and the same history.

According to the analysis of Mahamadou Sangare, professor at the high school of Sikasso (Mali), "The cultural identity is an anthropological concept that designates a historic period during which a community, a people, recognizes itself, by precise values in his practices, his concepts, his thoughts, his art, etc."

So cultural identity defines itself in time and in space because the values that determine it have a dynamic character, which evolve over time. One would not know how to mention with precision and exhaustive way the values that permit the identity of a people in one moment in history.

For Africa, a mosaic of peoples and communities that share a recent past marked by slavery and colonization would not know how to brag today about an authentic African culture expressing its identity again.

However, hope is permitted. The possibilities of a reconquest of our identity exist. The African languages, the set of the units of the language either spoken or written proper to a community, the language being this faculty that we have to communicate between us and to express our thoughts.

Africa counts more than a thousand languages, so Africa would be the continent that counts more languages with a strong density in sub-Saharan Africa.

In most cases, they are practiced only by some villages and even often by only one; in spite of this obvious diversity, some real affinities exist between most of these languages. All these languages would drift in a small number among them.

The reconquest of the African cultural identity passes therefore by an epistemological and historic survey of the African languages. All African languages make reference to literary shapes, symbolisms, and techniques of production of goods and services.

The language founds the cultural identity. Thus, the language is the pillar of the culture. To this topic, I would allow myself to mention an eminent specialist of the African culture, the Malian Seydou Badian Kouyaté, who said, "By the language, we have what the past let us like message and what the present composes for us. It is the language that binds us, and it is her that founds our identity. She is an essential element and there is not a culture without language. The language helps us to interpret all."

Africa would not know how to avoid exchanging with the other continents. Our identity would express itself better through a real opening on the other continents today because their influence on our languages are irreversible (slavery and colonization oblige). Here it would be necessary to recall the epigones and the detractors of the African identity.

During the period of colonization and even after, the school was the only reference in the education and the formation of the children. Domestic education was banished to the last plan, our parents being considered like savages. All children who had the luck to go to school were taught only by the school. They had separated thus and progressively of their cultural root.

The programs taught to this time, alas even currently again in most cases, could not take in account the cultural factors of our surroundings because they were based on foreign models, transporting a foreign culture to our local realities. Our only historic and cultural references were strangers, ours being only of bloodthirsty and savages, they said. Consider the release of the book *Negroes Nation and Culture* by Cheikh Anta Diop, and how very few African intellectuals dared to adhere to it. It took twenty years before a part of the ideas of Cheikh A. Diop were officially recognized at the international level at the time of the international symposium of Cairo of 1974, initiated by UNESCO and uniting the most eminent Egyptologists from all over the world. In short, at the time, the thought of this valorous person of Africa provoked extremely controversial reactions.

To understand the significance of the work of Cheikh A. Diop, it's first of all essential to know where the thought and the historic conscience of Cheikh A. Diop entered in the scientific field can understand itself on one hand by the dominant philosophical and anthropological currents, of the other by the history of the report that the West maintained with African.

In this context, let's mention philosopher G. W. Hegel (1770–1831), who maintained that Africa was the only continent without history, because it never produced something that one could call "civilization." According to Hegel, Egypt was part of Asia, and the history of humanity moved from the east to the west, avoiding the African continent (cf. Van Grassdorf, 2003:64).

To name some other influential thinkers only, let's mention Arthur of Gobineau (1816–1882) of which his work of reference (*Test on the Inequality of the Races*) constituted the ideological basis of colonization and the big racist theories (cf. Gnonsea, 2003s). In the institutional setting, it is necessary to mention the Institute of Technology of France, created in 1925 by Lucien Levy-Bruhl, where it was taught that the blacks had a "prelogique mentality." The theoreticians applied this to legitimize, to the philosophical and ethnological plan, the intellectual inferiority enacted of the Negro. The vision of an Africa, historic and atemporal, of which the inhabitants, the Negroes, were never responsible, by definition, of only one fact of civilization, imposed itself henceforth in the writings and anchored in the consciences (cf. Obenga, 1981). According to Cheikh A. Diop, the theories of the history of Africa served colonialism: Their goal was to make believe that the blacks always lived under the domination of the whites and that it was never responsible for whatever happened at home (cf. 1975:14 and 31).

With regard to the historic report between the West and Africa, it was always bound in a dynamic manner to the racist theories. The words, the pictures, the intellectual and political ideas can be discerned as the nonmaterial side of the real and material relations (cf. Guillaumn, 1992s). This very known relation is marked by five centuries of deletion and destruction of the African population, her culture, and her economy by the slave trade, the missionary work, and colonialism. At the same time as the Europeans developed a conviction of superiority and mission thanks to their success and their conquests, the Africans lost the conscience of their rich history and developed a sense of inferiority. The missionary work, the military violence, and the repressive school system made the Africans internalize the idea that before the arrival of the Europeans, they lived in a wild world that was barbarian and atheistic. Therefore, the history of Africa would only have begun with colonization. This conscience of inability and incompetence led to the belief that only the whites can find some solutions to the problems of Africa and prevented a self-determined development henceforth (cf. Ndumbe, 2002:4-7). Cheikh A. Diop expressed this cultural alienation as follows: "The cultural poison, inoculated learnedly since the most tender childhood, became integral part of our substance and appeared in all our judgments" (1975:15).

The black peoples can themselves also create their own language, their own alphabet, and their own universities to train their own physicians, their own engineers, and so on. I am certain that they have the means, when I think about all its artists, sportsmen, and captains of industry who wonder today where to invest their millions that go moldy in the bank. Can they contribute to the historic unification of the black peoples before the end of their days, getting their names engraved on the board of history? Most certainly that's a yes. As a Malian proverb says it: "When a goat is present one must not bleat to its place!" Indeed, one too often lends, to the blacks, intentions that are not theirs. One interprets the customs or traditions according to a logic that, without stopping being logical, is not theirs. The differences of psychology and understanding distort the interpretation being born of the outside. Here, I attempt to put in evidence the genesis and the dynamics of the necessity of an universal unification of the black peoples.

Although times are not the same anymore, I think that my ideas are stimulating to understand and to fight the marginalizing of the black peoples in the efficient management of our contemporary societies. It's a very present interest to attempt to determine what can incite to attract the consciences of the black peoples to adhere without conditions to my noble ideal. I know others will blame me for the superficiality of the approach, the redundancy of a reflection already outlined to see, to take the writer's setting that is above all to transmit fundamental values in accessible narration to a large readership, that is yet the essential message of this present writing, that doesn't stop, however, from making the sifter of the present pass one of the biggest topics of my generation.

The African cultural potentialities are always in a raw state and express a pressing need of refinement. If the West could grant its attention such as oil, gold, and diamonds, a lot of discoveries would have been made to the profit of humanity as whole.

All this leads to believing that before the end of this century, the tendency will reverse itself in favor of Africa because soon there won't be any more oil in the Middle East and there won't be any more gas in Europe. During this time in Africa, from Mount Nimba (Guinea), to Kilimanjaro (Tanzania), all mining fortunes, all oil-bearing waits the auspicious moment to propel toward a lasting cultural and economic progress. To be interested in the vitality of Africa is to know how to push its pawn on a chessboard, the continent being called to term to become the first world economic power. However, all is not shiny in this old Africa within, which the social inequalities continue to play a negative role, the upsurge of communal confrontations, and especially of the condition of women, which continues to undergo a particularly devouring discrimination. In such a context of aggravation of inequalities, the fight looks long and biting. Far from wanting to fight against the traditions, it seems, however, important and otherwise indispensable to me to denounce in a high voice their complicity in the discrimination of women.

The African writers invested in the right to speak the truth must, at any price, fight against the refusal of the right to the expression of which some African women undergo unjustly: the taboos, the superstition, the polygamy, the tribalism. How can a woman bloom when she's constantly obliged to fight against her rivals to keep her husband's affection? How can one raise as one hears its own children, when one must accept the will of the elders? How can you stand back and think in a quiet moment, when the custom obliges you to live with ten or twenty under the same roof? This practice probably represents an abuse of the traditional values of fraternity and generosity, because it slows down all individual projects. You cannot save your money, nor to make personal projects, because you're submitted to the requirement of the group. The man's "gregarious" perception that takes root in the traditional culture doesn't conceive the individual's existence outside of the community. However, it's precisely in the individuality that resides the source of progress.

By literature rather than by its semblance, the African writers must denounce the psychological conditioning of women and the limitation of feminine individuation in social ethics.

Africa must make itself ready to become the first world economic power. The political greediness of her leaders, which cheats with the rules of democracy to maintain them lifelong in power, constitutes a serious handicap for the advent of the African progress. How can a president who assumes more than five terms speak of democracy? The African presidential regimes are the monarchies that never say their names; it's a real political hypocrisy.

According to Professor Juma of Harvard University, "Democracy is in trouble in Africa. Although most of the dictators are gone, ethnic supremacy and other sectarian forces are taking their place. This apparent reversal of democracy is a sign of the limits of the negative kind of democracy that is focused only on removing the ravages of arbitrary power.

"Africa needs positive democracy, one that strengthens the capacity of the people to control their own destiny. More specially, government programs need to be guided by smart party platforms that articulate people's welfare. Without such institutions, the political and economic gains made so far will be eroded by ethnic and sectarian rivalries.

"The removal of dictators and the holding of regular elections have not been accompanied by the creation of institutions that allow the population to have a say in programs for their own welfare."

Another very negative aspect that this awareness must stop is the diffusion of bad pictures of Africa by the humanitarian organizations with a goal of raising money; one can help without disparaging. There are also the different marvels of the other Africa, not the selfish Africa that shows through the media, where one only sees poor children with distended stomachs. In the West, one doesn't know Africa or about the villages and the horrors of armed conflicts. Yet Africa is not only that; there's another life in society that the Westerners envy about Africa.

Africa is a rich continent but the bad management of its resources and corruption constitute serious constraints to the continent's development. With the free partnership swapping that weakened her and that made of her a market where one pours Western products, she doesn't have the possibility to have a competitive industry in terms of free total exchange.

Africa is involved in a system that she doesn't know and doesn't even master, the system of others, that means a merely Western system. The West conceived this economic and political system in accordance with the realities of its environment. Africa is landed therefore in this system that, without being adapted to its own realities, will never be able to bring him the socioeconomic progress that his peoples expect. Therefore, Africa should try to innovate his own development realities before borrowing those of the others.

Vector of the universal civilization, Africa, if she was not dispossessed of her creative virtues, could have continued to preserve her faculties of invention because it is her first that God, the all powerful, predestined this divine privilege. To glimpse the future economic and social progress of Africa seems for others to be merely something abstract, perhaps even simply a dream. However, Africa in full mutation, although confronted with multiple challenges, foretells, nevertheless, a best future whether we believe it or not. The continent's emerging and potential oil and gas resources should not be taken lightly. Countries like Nigeria, Equatorial Guinea, Algeria, and Egypt, all of which are experiencing rapid growth, and Mauritania and Guinea Republic are breaking new frontiers in exploration activities. For Namibia, a country without a record of commercial oil production, the Sandton Convention Center, venue of the eighteenth World Petroleum Congress (WPC), provided a window to shop for ways to develop its offshore gas reserves.

Nigeria, the continent's leading oil producer, also found the WPC a perfect platform to use to market its abundant oil and gas potentials.

Described as the last emerging market, it would have been a mistake for the organizers of the World Petroleum Congress to continue to ignore Africa. Happily, that has not been the case. For the first time in seventy-two years, all roads led to Africa, as the eighteenth World Petroleum Congress, which takes place every three years, was held in Johannesburg, South Africa, in September 2005.

With new discoveries being made virtually every day and the scramble for marginal fields gaining new impetus, oil-producing African countries could not have found a better chance to showcase the opportunities that abound in their respective territories.

In every point of view Africa is, and remains, the future world attic. She must simply put back the order on the vital questions that are between other civil peace and management of the national resources.

Africa is trying to come out of a long period of decline that covers several centuries and whose strong moments are the slave trade and colonization. She wishes to accomplish the beneficial jump into a modernity that for a long time had been made inaccessible without taking impetus. Very sure, a simple reappraisal of our history will allow us to give an account that in the past centuries the African societies didn't enjoy, that is neither peace nor development. But our consolation for this time being is nevertheless of size: These societies had the possibility to invent their future, to initiate the political solutions to their problems as illustrated eloquently in a variety of state-controlled models and constant redefinition that they underwent. It's true that history is not susceptible to bring solutions already made to the problems that arise to the present, but it participates in their invention.

Here the dominant idea is the rehabilitation of Africa, the continent that didn't finish to emerge from the darkness of slavery and colonialism. It's necessary that the African writers denounce with strength and oratory the crimes of slavery and colonialism, and that they exalt the liberating fight, of which one of the dramatic episodes constitutes the plot: Senegalese Skirmishers of the World War II battlefront were murdered in mass in the camp of Thiaroye-on-sea in Dakar just for asking for their savings, which the military authorities decided to divert to their own ends.

The vast continent of Africa is so rich and diverse in its culture, not only changing from one country to another but within an individual country, many different cultures can be found. When it comes to the oral tradition, its content is characterized by diversity, and the fable is the most known of the African oral tradition. It's generally defined as a narration of imaginary adventures to didactic vocation. It's popular, which means created by and for the people: It's born and lives by the collaboration between the people listening and the respected storyteller of his ideology, of his culture. Traditionally, it is transmitted orally from generation to generation. It depends closely on the culture and the people's physical geography that produced it. It is generally told to the young by the old, at dusk. Among the numerous explanations for the time of enunciation of the tale, let's keep the one here: "The night is more auspicious to the dream and to the creative imagination, and the mind is more free after work and the diurnal worries."

Finally, the African oral tradition is the expression of a traditional life. It covers different kinds that go from the myth to the epic while passing by the tales, the fables, the riddles, and the proverbs. She treats social, cultural, political, and economic structures of the African traditional society. The fable doesn't defer the tale so. It's an imaginary or mythological narration intended to illustrate a perception.

The narration, often short and humorous, can be assimilated to an anecdote. The myth is a long narration that is an object of strong belief for the people that produced it. Indeed, different from the tale, in which the sharing of the real has the tendency to balance itself, the myth is bound intimately to the occult. In the traditional Africa, the myth begins to sacredness itself, it can be considered like a legend. It has been reserved to chosen audiences, to circles of insiders, a long time until the disappearance of his religions to which he was bound.

The epic narration relates the exploits of a hero who really existed and who played a major role in the history of a people or an ethnic group. It also translates the exploits of a historic character or a caste.

For centuries, some of these songs, such as the Douga of the Guinean Malinke tribe who's traditional Region is the Manding, kept their character. They were only begun on particular occasions and could not be danced to simply when people wanted it. Sometimes they were connected to mythical characters, legendary or historic; they had, in the Manding philosophy, eponym value and were surrounded by many taboos. However, these airs, by their plasticity, can be adapted to other characters.

Genealogies are the recalled history of a dynasty, of a people. Intended to please, the epic and genealogies are often sung by the Griot or are said to the sound of an instrument of music. They can provide the numbers and dates to the historians, as well as lists of names.

The proverbs are vivid truths to which the tale most often serves as an illustration. Some storytellers say the proverb before developing it with the help of the tale. The proverbs are often told to the young by the old, who like nowadays again to decorate their speech with it: They connote the oratory and wisdom.

Here are some proverbs from the Malinke tribe:

- A friendship is close to fissure as soon as you note that your friend's garment is carried by your enemy. (Where mistrust begins, the friendship finishes.)
- Only one finger cannot collect the stone.
- Water your beard when fire burns the one of your neighbor.
- You take care of the pains of someone's teeth, and it's the one that will finish to crunch your seed of peanuts!
- One cannot know when the fisher urinates in the river!
- Did the goat pass; did the hyena pass; if the goat gets lost, who is to interrogate?
- To be a friend to a red monkey is beneficial in this sense, that one will know how to climb on a tree!
- If you burst the child's eyes while summoning him the order not to reveal it at the village, his burst eyes will!
- If you know where to go, the night doesn't find you on the way! (It's good to have time before oneself.)
- You warm yourself, to old age, with wood that you bought in youth!
- The cutting blade of your father, the cutting blade of your mother, your own cutting blade is the best!
- The spouse says "my child"; the wife says my "child"; each one is right!

- If you make of your child an Imam, you will pray behind him!
- The tail of a monkey is long, but if you have it clipped, it hurts him. (If you hurt my child, it hurts me.)
- Before lying down you must sit first. (Before harvesting you must sow first.)

The riddles and the enigmas are a kind of "game of hide-and-seek by speech" that are delivered by grandparents and grandchildren. In some societies, they are practiced exclusively between youngsters.

The songs occupy an important place in the index of the African oral literature. Some even define the song as being "the adornment" of the verb. The songs intervene to every moment of life, especially on the occasion of ritual ceremonies (crops, circumcisions, etc).

African songs reflect the state of Africa. There is amazing diversity but it is divided and full of paradox. The words uttered back in 1997 by Cameroonian saxophonist Manu Dibango still ring true today: "An impatient and bold youth cohabits, often awkwardly, with music traditions and beliefs that remain steadfast; musicians continue to play a vital role in daily life yet are hampered by a lack of structure and the corrosive factor of piracy, and female artists chip away at the patriarchal music community, proving they are a potent force for the future."

The crowning of one of Africa's greatest-ever musicians, and his death a month later, was a great loss for the continent. Ali Farka Touré was the continent's first artist to win two U.S. Grammy awards in a remarkable career that saw him composing and recording until practically his last breath. The Malian guitarist had worked his way up from illiterate trucker to globally recognized blues man. For many, Touré epitomized cultural independence and pride in the face of a Western music invasion. He took blues back to its birthplace. In 2005,

K'Naan, a Somalian rap sensation, became his country's first artist ever to be featured on MTV. And, as a mayor of his town, Niafunke mixed politics and music, reaffirming the traditional role of the African Griot. He mixed wisdom and entertainment to pass on his message.

Born in New York thirty-one years ago, hip hop hybrids are spawning fascinating music revivals in countries like Angola, Guinea, and Kenya, nations that had been musically moribund for decades. Like all rebel youth music, its most fertile ground has been in impoverished urban zones, where day-to-day survival is often dogged by conflict.

According to the International Federation of Hip Hop, Conakry (Guinea) and Dakar (Senegal) are third and fourth, respectively, in world rankings for the number of rap bands they host.

Despite political instability and the country's chronic economic woes, the music scene in Guinea continues to show a vitality also reflected by its female artists. The Ideal Black Girls were in the line-up of the continent's first women's rap festival while, on the other side of the generational scale, Africa's most famous female band, Les Amazones de Guinée, reunited to record their second album in forty-four years.

South Africa has also seen its hip hoppers explore uncharted territory. As its heroes of the past, Miriam Makeba and Hugh Masekela, enter the twilight of their careers, a new generation of township rap has surfaced.

This music is somewhere between indigenous kwaito, new-school, and house music.

The International Hip Hop Federation should immediately implement a policy of "no one left behind" in order to assist these struggling artists and to implement hip hop around the world. In my own judgment, hip hop is a real tool of expression through which black people can pass their messages, long blocked by political supremacy and the crippling realities of black people's day-to-day survival.

Hip hop is becoming a universal song that consolidates the cultural tie between black people from all over the world. Henceforth, it can be transmitted from generation to generation. There should be an International Hip Hop Cultural Center that gathers hip hop artists from all over the world every five years to compete, to exchange, and to create.

In Africa, the transmission of the tradition is the business of everybody, especially if it must reverberate on the education of the children. This is how the near family is implied in the process of transfer of the knowledge for the same reason as the Griots, true professionals of the speech, but also the storytellers, the singers, or the African writers who, a little later, endeavored to integrate the tradition in their works.

Very frequently in Africa, it's the father who instructs his son and the mother, her daughter. In some societies, the maternal uncle plays a more important role than the father with the boy, this one being more free with him than with his father and questioning him more gladly.

The young boy who comes with his father or his uncle to the field, to hunt or to go fishing, and the little girl who helps her mother, who goes with her to the well, receive not only technical instruction but all sorts of information on the natural habitat or the social life. The pretext is generally found in the task that they are accomplishing or in meetings made on the way. The grandparents, anxious to ensure the continuity of the tradition, always appear available to transmit their knowledge. It's they who are incumbent upon the transmission of the tradition to the children according to wisdom procured by age. By a psychological game, they always manage to put the children at ease and to motivate them to listen attentively. They appear everywhere as important educational agents in the domains that didn't directly milk the productivity, and in particular in the oral teaching.

They always make the distinction between those that deserve to be brought to the attention of the children and those which, by their nature and their effects, deserve to be kept secret until the children reach the adult age. Their role is not at all negligible as regards to the actual social integration.

They act as a hyphen between the past and the present. It's often at them that are going to live in the small child after the severance or when, four years, he begins to see the things and to ask some questions. In Africa, the children and their grandparents behave as cousins. One notices that contrary to the relation that binds them to their parents, with their grandparents they are characterized by a sort of equality, of connivance, of tacit alliance, of propensity to the joke.

However, the children always know the limit of their free space, of the things that they can allow and cannot allow with grandparents. It's the grandmother who is the most competent in the oral transmission of knowledge; she has a lot more free time. Indeed, in all societies, the grandmother is this character characterized by a big tolerance, a human experience that makes the "human library" of it. She occupies a place of choice in the conservation of the traditional values. In the traditional Africa, the grandmother was the only one authorized to speak overtly of sex to the children, who benefited from this to put all sorts of questions.

It agrees, however, to note that in Africa, all old men can intervene in the transmission of the tradition, whether he is the insider's big parent or not. The aged characters are always sources available that, free of the daily chores, can put their experience and their memory to the service of the education of the children.

Professionals of speech, the Griot has been considered at all times as the possessor of the speech, therefore the social memory of the group. He keeps the facts and the events important of its time but also of the past times, that his fathers confided to him so that he restores them to the future generations. This is how, real professional of the speech, the Griot looks after their good transmission. One calls on him at the time of the important events during which he always makes himself available to reconstitute the genealogy of a family given to the sound of the "kora" or another instrument of music according to the type of society. Periodically, big meetings of esoteric characters, gathered by the Griots, are initiated for summing up the history of the people. At the time of these ceremonies, the youngsters among them acquire new knowledge. The eldest present them the consecrated sites, tombs, or former altars, and teach them the systems of deduction of the time for every ethnic group, and the old shapes of the languages that allow the chiefs of the subgroups to understand themselves.

Other agents that intervene in the transmission of the oral tradition are the storytellers, who always have some messages to transport at the time of the nocturnal vigils, but also the singers, who draw at will in the national index.

In my country, the Republic of Guinea, more precisely in High Guinea (The Manding) , poetry is a respected profession and insures the Griot in such a way he can disembark in any meeting and utter everything that comes into his head with impunity. His performance will even rate him a tip, which he asks for, the rest with an aggressive greed achieves, in the tones of the nightmare and the caricature, the dream of the almighty verb. His speech assigns to the things and the beings their just place; without it the universe would dissolve itself in chaos.

In spite of this demiurgical role, the Griot endures all his life a unanimous contempt. At his death, one won't bury his cadaver, whose impurity would contaminate the earth; the hollow tree trunk will serve him for burial. Such facts existed not long ago in High Guinea, in the Malinke region that sits astride the border of Guinea and Mali.

There was the center of the medieval empire of Mali, and in the nineteenth century, Samory Touré established his kingdom there, the Griot I have just presented under a bad day, that is, the "Dyéli," formed one of the castes of the former hierarchy Malinké. Unlike the other hierarchical occupations (blacksmiths, tailors of wood, shoemakers), they don't produce anything tangible. They work on wind. Authors, speakers, singers, musicians, mimes, dancers, depositories of the oral traditions, their profession consists in manipulating some signs. The survey of the strict disciplines of memory and improvisation specializes them since childhood in the aesthetic use of the language. These are of the professionals of speech, of which they modulate resources with a fabulous aptitude. Who had luck to follow, in one of these villages, the lines of working drawing that bloom the high valleys of Niger, the performance of an experienced Griot, keep the intuition of the report between the artistic achievement and the technical efficiency? This one discerned through the effects of the speech, or rather of the total spectacle, on the assembly: There appears the sovereign power of the style.

The Malinke society ensures its Griots complete freedom of speech. No topic is forbidden to them; all is allowed. This faculty that they have to translate "made emotional " any experience that drives them to magnify all passions, even those that, like lust or drunkenness, challenge the established morals. Challenge living generosities of those that he shocks, artist curses exhibiting itself in the official ceremonies, the Griot offers a lot of features that relate it to one lineages of European literature, the one that goes from the Arétin to the surrealists.

More rational, however, than their Nordic equivalent, the institutions of this country guarantee to the Griots an absolute impunity. So serious the offensive, so shameless against truth, no one can castigate it, nor even reprimand it. In case of war, and if the fate turns, the loser's Griot will pass (without sentence) to the winner's service. Delegated to speech, he occupies an untouchable position and has since he agrees to take this term to the letter. The immunity of which it arranges matches logically of their political and military inability. The Griot cannot exercise a function of authority; nor does he have the right to carry weapons.

All happens as if his share, the mastery of the verb, made him unfit to intervene directly in human business. Since he speaks, he would not know how to act. The interpretation of these data stumbles on a double difficulty. How first to understand that the function of speech is thus devolved to a specialized group? How does he, himself, make sure that this group benefited from such privileges, while breathing such an indignity?

During social events organized by the Guinean communities in the United States, one wonders about how they, in spite of their relative ease, sometimes even superior to the other, don't hesitate to brave their origins, their profession of Griot to benefit from the generosity of their fellow citizens with enthusiasm and pride. It is really there that we come to the evidence of the incontestable vivacity of the African traditions and their cultural values.

The attitude of children with regard to the oral tradition was very positive in traditional Africa. The social organization of that Africa was more in favor of the transmission of the oral tradition and the interest of the children for these traditions.

The traditional society is very different from the modern society. The first is characterized by the mind of the group, while individualism, an immediate consequence of urbanization, rages in the second. Indeed, the bursting of the widened families, the eruption of the Western life-styles (school), the modern transmission channels of information (the media) are many elements that participate in the disappearance of the phenomenon. There are no more Griots bound to families or clans to enliven the vigils, nor nearly more of kassaks, nor of sacred woods, and so on. So the African child should be content that a grandmother, if he has luck to have one in the domestic house, is able to well tell to him, between learned two lessons. But the majority of the children, once the lessons are learned and after-school chores are done, prefer to watch television or to play with the neighbors.

The oral tradition inspired the African authors a lot. Indeed, a number of them make a big place more and more, for the oral tradition that always has a didactic range.

Indeed, from the tale to the myth, while passing by the proverbs and riddles and until the epic narrations, there is always a teaching to pull, a value to instill in the child.

The themes of instruction are provided more for the tales and the proverbs. The symbolic significance emanating from these two kinds is used on several plans: knowledge of the nature, morals, social behavior, and so on.

The heroes of the tales are evidence of a system of values and embody, following the cases, the virtues that lead them to the social success or the shortcomings that drive them to their loss. The traditional African tales often put on the stage, animals and the qualities that one wants to instill in the children, such as the following:

- The indispensable prudence to their survival, good memory, generosity, and modesty.
- The ruse under a shape or another—because she is indispensable to defend themselves against the brutal and harmful strengths of the environment.

- A good understanding of the society in which they are called to live, notably the attitudes and behaviors of his members.
- Dignity.

While growing, children better understand this sort of convenient morals illustrated by the tales. The children integrate these values without debating them so much that they are very young.

In the same way, one notes that the proverbs have their roots in the tradition that observes, explains, and interprets the facts, the rules of nature, and human behavior to express the social relations. They pull their value of the society that elaborates, herself, her rules of conduct and resists all change strongly.

The riddles also play an important role in the child's formation. They test his level of intelligence. Indeed, "the riddle is not a problem that one solves to help the data provided by the statement, because to some, there is not anything to guess but to know."

The epic doesn't escape the rule. Long and bewitching, often punctuated with songs, the epic narrations as exalting the action of the heroes give life to a people's history, and instill to the child the notions of courage and devotion in the community.

The popular songs constitute an abundant literature. The African peoples are excellent singers: They sing the plainest fact as the most extraordinary fact. The proof is that Africa provided great artists, singers of international fame, such as Soundjoulou Cissoko, Kouyate Sory Kandia, Lucky Doubey, Oum Khaltoum, to mention only those. Rich and very varied, these songs privileged to galvanize, to rally, or to mobilize the human energies, to reinforce the union and the peace between the social layers of the continent; they serve to express with oratory the feelings and the resentments that the African peoples feel in their life, in their history. Song of jubilation, song of lyric poets or of love, song satirical, they go from the simple nursery rhymes or lullabies that amuse the children.

In my country, Guinea, this kind is especially known in the Sudanese zone, represented by the High Guinea (The Manding). His populations, of origin and culture Manding, kept the essentials of the culture inherited from the big empires of the Middle Ages. The birth of these big political wholes on the ruins of micro-states to essentially tribal or cliquish character had encouraged the mixture of the culture and the values of civilization.

The castes see the day. With them, of the instruments of music, airs, and the famous songs. These instruments of music such as the "bolon", the "kora", the "balafon", improve, and new roles are assigned to them. Other mythical instruments destined to religious ceremonies, animists, some as the "balafon", wins the royal court to rock the king and his court. And the function of Griot, by example, codifies itself and institutionalizes himself. She will consist in archiving in the memory, the history of the people of Manding, to counsel the king, while calling on deep knowledge of the society. In this work, the Griot will make itself come with his instrument of music, the "kora" or the "balafon".

Still in the setting of the oral tradition, let's analyze "Farakouroun," the hymn of the blacksmiths, of the Manding in High Guinea. It would be difficult, or even impossible, to give with certainty the period of birth of this song. Several informants say it was born in the time of Glory of the Empire of Mali, that means the thirteenth or fourteenth century. Others say it goes back to a more recent period. Whatever one tells to some, we are tempted to situate its origins in the time of the division of the Mandings' society in body of professions and castes, to the same moment that the hymns of the Griots, of the hunters, and others. She was begun during the big ceremonies, of the reunions on the occasion of the death of a big personality, to magnify the work of the blacksmith.

Only these last were allowed then to dance it. This dance is even executed nowadays, and is made of characteristic footsteps. The young blacksmiths, an ax in their hand, show evidence of agility and dexterity while juggling with their weapons. . The children mime their gestures behind the bellows, also designated the forge.

Nowadays, this dance has the tendency to disappear. However, the song "Farakouroun" continues to hold in suspense the young of the villages during the vigils. The song is translated as follows:

Move you, Farakouroun,

Transform iron, tin, bronze, and gold,

Beat money, lead, and iron,

Farakouroun, nor the hoe, nor the ax,

Cannot get themselves

Without you, point of plow, of knife.

Beloved spouse of Nounfadima,

Beloved spouse of Nounyalen,

Raise you, agitate you, Farakouroun.

Raise you that I sing you this air.

Raise you that I sing you Farakouroun,

Farakouroun, the song of the blacksmiths,

Of the Manding.

Raise you, striking, beat and transform.

Farakouroun, move you,

Without you point of hoe, of knife,

Dance, dance your air, Farakouroun,

Blacksmith of the Manding.

It is your hymn,

The hymn of the Masters of fire and the iron

Of the Manding.

It's therefore obvious that oral tradition plays an important role in the transmission of knowledge. This role is conferred by the fact that it's impregnated deeply in the cultural realities and the social values. However, do all these values find their place in the modern society?

At this stage, the question that it agrees to land is, what is the future for the oral traditions? Do the oral traditions belong to the past, or can they cohabit on the contrary with the modern, cultural, scientific world?

Modern society is characterized by a scientific development, a technological progress incontestable, and of the new attitudes: the desire to look for, to pass itself, to innovate, to deeply immerse oneself for pure intelligence. Individualism rages in urban environments, which doesn't facilitate the transmission of values transported by the oral traditions at all. Even in the countries where the immigration toward the cities or besides has subtly modified the former order of things. Henceforth, most such elements of the oral tradition genealogies, the mottos belong to folklore, and its values are more and more disconnected from reality.

Circumcision, for example, lost its ritual initiation, to be only a hygienic precaution, and in some localities, there is the opportunity to recover the former modes of circulation of goods and to rejoin the community in gigantic feasts.

In short, the cultural cohabitation of traditional and modern becomes more and more unlikely, the second having taken advantage of the first. However, can one pass to the sifter the values transported by the oral traditions in order to see those that center more with the needs of the present society?

Finally, it would be necessary to succeed in not representing the oral tradition as the only support of our societies, but to show that there were also the acquirements and the technical innovations very adapted to the soils and the needs of the humans of that period of time , and that one must protect, discuss, and transpose. It's to this level that the modern pedagogue must fear it and try to capture strengths and the wealth that the oral tradition contains again to associate them to his own methods.

Africa is home to innumerable tribes and ethnic and social groups, some representing very large populations consisting of millions of people. Others are smaller groups of a few thousand. All these tribes and groups have cultures which are different, but represent the mosaic of cultural diversity of Africa.

There are many different groups and tribes across the continent of Africa with their culture varying from tribe to tribe. Such tribes and ethnic/social groups include the following:

AFAR

The Afar people live primarily in Ethiopia (Danakil desert) and the areas of Eritrea, Djibouti, and Somalia in the eastern part of Africa. They keep cows, sheep, and goats for meat and milk, and donkeys, horses, and camels for transport. A man's wealth is assessed by his animals.

ANYI

The Anyi people live in the southeastern part of Ivory Coast (West Africa). The language spoken is (Akan cluster of Twi). The rise of the early Akan centralized states began in the thirteenth century and may be related to the opening of trade routes established to move gold throughout the region. The Anyi people are a subgroup of the Akan, who migrated to their current location from what is present-day Ghana between the sixteenth and eighteenth centuries. They were never as powerful as the Ashanti and Baule and, as a result, were indirectly under their rule during the height of both empires. Anyi agricultural economy revolves around banana and taro production. Yams are also an important staple crop in the region. Many locally grown crops were introduced from the Americas during the Atlantic slave trade.

Ashanti

The Ashanti people live in southern Ghana (West Africa). Their spoken language is (Akan cluster of Twi). At the end of the seventeenth century, the grand Ashanti Kingdom emerged in the central forest region of Ghana, when several small states united under the Chief of Kumasi in a move to achieve political freedom from the Denkyira. It is said that the Golden Stool of the Ashanti descended from heaven to rest on the knees of Osei Tutu, the first Ashantehene, who was guided by his adviser, the priest Okomfe Anokye. The early Ashanti economy depended on the trade of gold.

Berber

The Berber people live in Morocco and other neighboring Saharan countries. The language spoken is Berber, and they have a population of 3 million. Berber history in North Africa is extensive and diverse. Their ancient ancestors settled in the area just inland of the Mediterranean Sea to the east of Egypt. Many early Roman, Greek, and Phoenician colonial accounts mention a group of people collectively known as Berbers living in northern Africa. Contrary to popular romanticism, which portrays Berbers as nomadic peoples crossing the desert on camels, most actually practice sedentary agriculture in the mountains and valleys throughout northern Africa.

Bobo

The Bobo people live in the western part of Burkina Faso and Mali, with a population of 110,000. The language spoken is Bobo (Mande). The Bobo have lived in the region for centuries, with some estimates dating back to AD 800. It's generally believed that they moved into this area from the north. One of the primary reasons for this thinking is that they speak a language considered to be part of the Mande family, which originates to the north in Mali. Farming among the Bobo is of primary importance. Agricultural activity is not merely a way of providing subsistence among the Bobo, it is the essential component of their day-to-day existence. The major food crops are red sorghum, pearl millet, yams, and maize.

Dogon

The Dogon are cliff-dwelling people who live in southeastern Mali and Burkina Faso. They are unique among groups in Africa, in that they have kept and continued to develop their culture even in the midst of Islamic invasions, which have conquered and adapted many other groups. Early history is informed by oral traditions, which claim that the Dogon originated from the west bank of the Niger River (tenth to thirteenth centuries). They emigrated west to northern Burkina Faso, where local histories describe them as *kibsi*. Around 1490, they fled a region, now known as the northern Mossi kingdom of Yatenga, when it was invaded by Mossi cavalry. They ended up in the Bandiagara cliffs region, safe from the approaching horsemen.

Fon

The Fon people live in southern Benin, Togo (West Africa). The Fon kingdom of Dahomey, which was ruled by the kings of the Alladahonu dynasty for over two hundred years, reached its political and economic peak between the early eighteenth and the mid-nineteenth centuries. After conquering numerous small coastal states, the income helped to support the wealth of the king, whose power was absolute. The Fon king was defeated by the French in 1892, and in 1894, the area now known as Benin became a colony of France, under the name of Dahomey. The primary cash crops in this region are yams, cotton, and taro, but the Fon also grow sorghum, sesame, millet, palms, maize, and okra, among other crops for local consumption.

Fulani

The Fulani people live in many countries such as Guinea-Conakry, Senegal, Mali, Burkina Faso, Nigeria, Niger, Cameroon, and Chad. Their spoken language is Pulaar, (Fulfulde). The Fulani, who are mainly nomadic, have been influential in regional politics, economics, and histories throughout western Africa for over a thousand years. They played a significant role in the rise and fall of the Mossi states in Burkina Faso and contributed to the migratory movements of people southward through Niger and Nigeria into Cameroon. They were also responsible for introducing and spreading Islam throughout much of western Africa. Fulani are herders and traders. The routes they established in western Africa provided extensive links throughout the region, which fostered economic and political ties between otherwise isolated ethnic groups. Dairy products produced from Fulani cattle were traded to sedentary farmers for agricultural products and luxury items.

Hamer

The Hamer people live in Ethiopia. Their spoken language is Hamer-Banna. They belong to a group of culturally distinct people known as the Sidamo. Although they are racially mixed with the Bushman hunters who originally inhabited the region, they do not have any Bushman features. Authorities agree that they are clearly a mixture of the Caucasian and Negroid races. Most of the Hamer are cattle breeders. They live in camps that consist of several related families. The families live in tents arranged in a circle, and the cattle are brought into the center of the camp at night. Herds belonging to the Hamer-Banna consist mainly of cattle, although there are some sheep and goats. Camels are used for riding and as pack animals. Most Hamer-Banna plant fields of sorghum at the beginning of the rainy season before leaving on their annual nomadic journey.

HAUSA.

The Hausa people live in northern Nigeria and the northwest of Niger Republic. Their spoken language is Hausa, with a population of 15 million people. The myths of origin among the Hausa say that their founder, Bayjidda, came from the east in an effort to escape from his father. He came thereafter to Gaya, where he used some blacksmiths to shape a knife for him. With his knife he continued to Daura, where he freed the people of the oppressive nature of a sacred snake that kept their wells and stopped them from getting water six days out of the week. Since the beginning of the history of Hausa, the seven states of Hausaland have been divided between activities of production and work according to their place and natural resources.

HUTU

The Hutu people live in Rwanda and Burundi (Central Africa). According to *Compton's Encyclopedia Online,* the Hutu were also called Bahutu or Wahutu, and are one of the three ethnic groups that make up the populations of Burundi and Rwanda. The Hutu number between 12 million and 13 million and represent about 90 percent of the population in Rwanda and about 85 percent of the population in Burundi. However, when the Hutu first arrived in Central Africa in the first century AD, they found it inhabited by the Twa. The Twa were Pygmy hunters who were forced to flee by the Hutu. Hutu life was based on the clan, with petty kings, also known as bahinza, ruling over limited domains. When the Tutsi arrived in the fourteenth or fifteenth century, the Hutu were subject to political and economic domination.

The majority of the Hutu population lives in rural areas in round grass huts on family farms, which are dispersed throughout the hills of Rwanda and Burundi. According to the *Anthropology Explorer* Web site, about one fourth of all Hutu follow native tribal religions; however, most of the Hutu are Roman Catholic. The Hutu speak the native languages of Kirundi in Burundi and Kinyarwanda in Rwanda. Those involved in trade also speak Swahili. The Hutu traditional activities include basket making, woodcarving, and metal work. Proverbs and songs also play an important part in Hutu culture.

Kikuyu

The Kikuyu tribe live in the Central Province of Kenya (East Africa). Having migrated to their current location about four centuries ago, the Kikuyu now make up Kenya's largest ethnic group. The Kikuyu spread rapidly throughout the Central Province of Kenya. The Kikuyu usually identify their land by the surrounding mountain range, which they call Kirinyaga, "the shining mountain." The Kikuyu are Bantu and actually came into Kenya during the Bantu migration. The Kikuyu tribe was originally founded by a man named Gikuyu. Kikuyu history says that the Kikuyu god, Ngai, took Gikuyu to the top of Kirinyaga and told him to stay and build his home there.

The Kikuyu rely heavily on agriculture. They grow bananas, sugarcane, arum lily, yams, beans, millet, maize, black beans, and a variety of other vegetables. They also raise cattle, sheep, and goats. In the Kikuyu culture, boys and girls are raised very differently. The girls are raised to work on the farm, and the boys usually work with the animals. The girls also have the responsibility of taking care of a baby brother or sister and also help the mother out with household chores.

Though they are traditionally agricultural people and have a reputation as hard-working people, a lot of them are now involved in business. Most of the Kikuyu still live on small family plots, but many of them have also seen the opportunities in business and have moved to cities and different areas to work. They have a desire for knowledge, and they believe that all children should receive a full education.

Kongo

The Kongo (a.k.a. the Bakongo) tribe live in southwestern Democratic Republic of Congo (formerly Zaïre), Angola, and Congo Republic. They are about 2 million people. Their spoken language is the Kikongo (central Bantou). The Kongo people emigrated to their current location during the thirteenth century from the northeast under the leadership of Wene. In 1482, the Portuguese arrived on the coast, and the Kongo began diplomatic relations, which included sending nobles to visit the Royal Assemblage in Portugal in 1485. Kongo leaders were targeted for conversion by Christian missionaries, often resulting in divisions between followers of Christianity and followers of the traditional religions. The Kongo people survive from day to day on agricultural production, fishing, and hunting. When the Kongo Kingdom was at its political apex in the fifteenth and sixteenth centuries, the king, who had to be a male descendant of Wene, reigned supreme.

Nzambi was the supreme god for all in the Kongo Kingdom, and the intermediary representations included land and sky spirits and ancestor spirits, all of whom were represented in *nkisi* objects. When an individual encountered hardship and feared that a spirit had been offended, it would be necessary to consult a diviner (*nganga*), who would often instruct the afflicted to add medicines to certain nkisi in order to achieve well-being.

Maasai

The Maasai tribe live in the north central part of Tanzania and the southern part of Kenya. They are about 350,000 people, and their language is Ol Maa (Nilotic). Maasai are the southern-most Nilotic speakers and are linguistically most directly related to the Turkana and Kalenjin, who live near Lake Turkana in west central Kenya. According to Maasai oral history and the archaeological record, they also originated near Lake Turkana. The Maasai are pastoralists and have resisted the urging of the Tanzanian and Kenyan governments to adopt a more sedentary life-style.

Maasai are best known for their beautiful beadwork, which plays an essential element in the ornamentation of the body. Cattle are central to the Maasai economy. They are rarely killed, but instead are accumulated as a sign of wealth and traded or sold to settle debts.

A cow is slaughtered as an offering during important ceremonies, marking completed passage through one age-grade and movement to the next. When warriors (*moran*) complete this cycle of life, they exhibit outward signs of sadness, crying over the loss of their youth and adventurous life-styles. Maasi diviners (*laibon*) are consulted whenever misfortune arises. They also serve as healers, dispensing their herbal remedies to treat physical ailments and ritual treatments to absolve social and moral transgressions.

Malinke

The Malinke tribe live in Guinea, precisely in the Niger plains of High Guinea (The Manding). The Malinke is a tribe entirely devolved to the traditional Africa. The Malinke oral tradition is very rich and deeply linked in the African history. They keep the best archives of the history of the African continent up to today.

Evoking the inheritance of his ancestors, the late Malinke writer Camara Laye said, "What our Mandingues ancestors bequeathed us, in this high Niger, is an ethics including loyalty, knighthood, respect of speech given that the Cola and the Kôra come with. Loyalty, respect of the speech given, the cola and the kôra must be kept. But one cannot play Samory in 1976. One cannot stop the sea with his arms. The knighthood is therefore a certain strength, very valid to the last century, but that one cannot oppose to the atomic bomb. It would agree therefore to convert it quickly and intelligently, this knighthood, in a strength of sympathy that, once free, will make our continent, not the earth of the antagonism but the continent of the reason and the balance."

The Malinkese are very bound and generally conservative. They are farmers and very gifted in the trade and traditional music. The first president of Free Guinea was Malinke, downward of the big warrior Samory Touré, who fought valiantly against colonization in West Africa.

The Malinke people are mostly Muslims.

MANDINGO

The Mandingo tribe live in Gambia and Casamance (Senegal). Mandingo people are big and tall, very dark-skinned, and very gifted fighters. They are mainly traders and well known as the best curators of traditional music.

MOSSI

The Mossi tribe live in central Republic of Burkina Faso. They are estimated to be 3.5 million people. The Mossi states were created about AD 1500, when bands of horsemen rode north from what is now northern Ghana into the basin of the Volta River and conquered several less powerful peoples, including Dogon, Lela, Nuna, and

Kurumba. These were integrated into a new society call Mossi, with the invaders as chiefs and the conquered as commoners. The emperor of the Mossi is the Moro Naba, who lives in the ancient and contemporary capital, Ouagadougou. The Mossi are primarily farmers, raising millet, sorghum, maize, sesame, peanuts, and indigo.

The descendants of the conquered farmers (*nyonyose*) honor nature spirits that provide them with supernatural power to control the weather, disease, crop failure, and general well-being. These are the "invented spirits" that become important as the congregation faces a particular affliction and which decrease in influence as the problem is solved. These spirits are often represented by masks and figures that make them visible and concrete.

Ngbaka

The Ngbaka tribe live in the northern Democratic Republic of Congo (formerly Zaire). The Ngbaka number about 400,000 people, and their native language is Gbaya (Ubangi). The Ngbaka arrived on the Gemena Plateau in 1920. They migrated from the area around Lake Chad to the north with the Manja and Gbaya peoples. The Ngbaka are primarily subsistence farmers who raise manioc and maize, along with sorghum and bananas. They also raise chicken and goats for eggs and milk. Most of the dietary protein comes from fish caught in the local rivers by women.

The blacksmith plays an important role in Ngbaka communities. He is responsible for fashioning many of the utilitarian objects that are necessary for farming, and he also makes arrowheads out of iron, which are used for the little hunting that is done.

Being able to trace one's lineage to an important or very old ancestor is the primary measure of political importance in Ngbaka villages. There is no centralized power representing all Ngbaka, but there is normally a headman in each village, who is selected and advised by individual family heads.

The Ngbaka believe in a supreme deity (Gale or Gbonboso). His message was brought to Earth by two messengers, Seto and Nabo, who are recognized as the primordial ancestors of the Ngbaka peoples.

PYGMIES (MBUTI)

Pygmy groups are scattered throughout equatorial Africa, from Cameroon in the west to Zambia in the southeast. In Zaire, there are three main groups of Pygmies: the Tswa in the west, the Twa between Lake Kivu and Lake Tanganyika, and the Mbuti (also referred to as Bambuti or BaMbuti) of the Ituri Forest. According to Turnbull, the most profound difference between the three groups is the linguistic difference, which is of recent origin and is purely "accidental" (Turnbull, 1965B:22-23). The Mbuti live in territorially defined nomadic bands. The membership of these bands is very fluid. Bands have no formal political structure; there are no chiefs, and there is no council. An informal consensus among old respected men is the basis of decisions affecting the entire camp. The Mbuti maintain relationships with surrounding village cultivators, whose language the Mbuti have adopted. Many accounts indicate that the Mbuti are highly acculturated and have adopted many features of villager life-style beyond language, such as the clan system and certain religious observances. Turnbull feels that these features are quite superficial, however.

The religious life of the Mbuti is not at all clear. Early reports state that they had no religion at all.
Source: Culture summary by Marlene M. Martin.

SENUFO

The Senufo tribe live in Mali and the northern part of Ivory Coast. Their spoken language is Senufo (Voltaic).

The Senufo are made up of a number of diverse subgroups, who migrated into their current location from the north during the fifteenth and sixteenth centuries. Unlike their neighbors to the north, they have remained relatively sheltered from intrusive cultures, including the Songhai and Hausa. Senufo agricultural products are typical of the region, including millet, sorghum, maize, rice, and yams. They also grow bananas, manioc, and a host of other crops that have been borrowed from cultures throughout the world. There are a number of revered ancestor and bush spirits among the Senufo. Maleeo and Kolotyolo ("Ancient Mother" and "Creator God") represent a dualistic deity. Kolotyolo is not approachable and can only be reached through Yiriigifolo or Nyebene. In the region of Kufulo, Maleeo is represented by the sacred drums, before whom all thieves and murderers are brought for trial.

Shilha Berbers

The Shilha tribe lives primarily in the beautiful, wooded High Atlas and Middle Atlas Mountains of Central Morocco. However, a large number of them also live on the slopes of the Atlas Mountains in eastern Algeria, near Morocco's border. They number about . 1.1 million

The central Shilha move their herds to the warm plains during the winter months, then to higher pastures during the spring and summer months. Depending on their locations in the mountains, some of the tribes only have to move their herds during the winter. Others only migrate during the summer. A third group moves the herds during the winter and the summer.

Although often on the move, none of the tribes are totally nomadic. All of them maintain permanent villages with fortified, community granaries and surrounding farmlands.

The villages are never left unattended. A small number of people stay behind to guard the granaries and to plant crops such as barley, maize, wheat, rye, millet, and vegetables.

Many central Shilha villages are found among the highest hills and are often built partially into the mountainsides. Very few villages have electricity or running water, but most have their own internal means of communication.

The central Shilha are 99.9 percent Muslim; however, their religious practices are based more on traditions and the decisions of the community judges than on the Quran. Most of the central Shilha have continued in their traditional worship of saints. One group of spiritual leaders, called *marabouts*, is considered "living saints." They are believed to possess healing abilities and supernatural powers. Each of the villages reveres one or more of these saints.

Credits: Christopher D. Roy, professor of the History of Art, the University of Iowa; also see credit page.

SWAHILI

The Swahili tribe live in coastal Kenya and Tanzania. Their native language is Kiswahili (Bantu). The inhabitants of the coastal areas of Kenya, Tanzania, and Mozambique share history, language, and cultural traditions, which some Swahili scholars claim date to at least AD 100, when an anonymous Greek traveler and author of the *Periplus of the Erytharaean Sea* wrote about a place in east Africa, which Arabs frequented to trade with those living on the mainland. This history is closely tied to Indian Ocean trade routes linking India, the Arabian Peninsula, and Africa. Swahili economy today, as in the past, is intricately linked to the Indian Ocean. For approximately 2,000 years, Swahili merchants have acted as middlemen between eastern and central Africa and the outside world. The Islam practiced by Swahili peoples is often very strict. Most of the requirements of the religion are practiced by many of the people. The economic success of the Swahili throughout the coastal region has encouraged many of their inland neighbors to adopt Islam as well.

Tuareg

The Tuareg tribe live in Niger, Mali, Senegal, Burkina Faso, and Nigeria. Their spoken language is Temajeg. "Tuareg" is a term used to identify numerous diverse groups of people who share a common language and a common history. Tuareg camel caravans played the primary role in trans-Saharan trade until the mid-twentieth century, when European trains and trucks took over. Tuareg history began in northern Africa, where their presence was recorded by Herodotus. Many groups have slowly moved southward. Today, many Tuareg live in sedentary communities in the cities bordering the Sahara that once were the great centers of trade for western Africa. For thousands of years, Tuareg economy revolved around trans-Saharan trade.

Most, if not all, Tuareg are followers of Islam. Among many Tuareg, this practice is nominal, and while daily prayers are made to Allah, strict adherence to other religious requirements is rare.

Wolof

The Wolof constitute a large ethnic group located mainly in the western part of the former French West African colony of Senegal, and extending southward into Gambia, the former British colony. "Wolof" ("Ouolof" in the standard French orthography) is the name by which the people refer to themselves, and the label is commonly used in scholarly publications. But a large number of orthographic variants occur in the literature, ranging from Chelofes, Guiolof, and Iolof, to Joloffs, Valaf, and Yuloff.

The indigenous language is also called Wolof. It is classified within the Northern Branch of the West Atlantic subfamily of the Niger-

Congo language family. The most closely related languages are Serer and Fulbe (Fulani) (Greenberg 1966: 7-8; 25; Voegelin 1977: 28-29). The Lebu, a separate ethnic group centered in the Cap-Vert peninsula of Senegal, speak a distinct Wolof dialect. The Wolof language is rapidly becoming the national vernacular of Senegal. Senegal is by far the most important national unit, since this is where approximately 95 percent of the Wolof are located. They constitute the dominant ethnic group in Senegal, both politically and numerically, as over one third of the national population.

The first solid documentary information on the Wolof dates from the travels of Ca da Mosto in 1455, but according to oral traditions, the Wolof ethnic group may have been in the process of formation sometime around the beginning of the thirteenth century. Probably during the fourteenth century, the Wolof were unified into a loose political federation known as the Djolof Empire, centered in northwestern Senegal.

The most fundamental basis of distinction among the Senegalese Wolof is the rural-urban differentiation.

The Wolof mainly occupy a tropical, semi-desert environment called the Sahel. Vegetation is sparse, and the topsoil consists of loose sand. The subsistence economy is based on agriculture, which in turn depends on rainfall, the key environmental factor. The basic subsistence crop and staple food is millet (primarily *Pennisetum gambicum*), while the main cash crop is peanuts (*Arachis hypogaea*). The second major foodstuff is rice, but it is not grown by most villagers and must be purchased.

The importance of Islam among the Wolof is indisputable.. In fact, it would be very difficult for a convert to Christianity to continue living in a Wolof village. The two dominant Muslim brotherhoods (*tariqas*) among the Wolof are the Tijaniyya and the Muriddiyya. Men become members of a brotherhood upon circumcision. They normally follow the brotherhood of their fathers. Women become members of a brotherhood upon marriage, joining the same one as their husbands.

The Wolof manifest a broad range of cultural variation and also share many cultural features with neighboring peoples such as the Lebu, Serer, and Tukulor.

Source: Culture summary by Robert O. Lagace.

YORUBA

The Yoruba tribe live in southwestern Nigeria and Benin. The language spoken is Yoruba. In the oral history of the Yoruba, an origin myth tells of God lowering a chain at Ile-Ife, down which came Oduduwa (the ancestor of all people), bringing with him a cock, some earth, and a palm kernel. The earth was thrown into the water, the cock scratched to become land, and the kernel grew into a tree with sixteen limbs, representing the original sixteen kingdoms. The Empire of Oyo arose at the end of the fifteenth century, aided by Portuguese guns. Expansion of the kingdom is associated with the acquisition of the horse. At the end of the eighteenth century, civil war broke out at Oyo, the rebels called for assistance to the Fulani, but the latter ended up conquering all of Oyo by the 1830s. The Fulani invasion pushed many Yoruba to the south, where the towns of Ibadan and Abeokuta were founded.

Historically, the Yoruba were primarily farmers, growing cocoa and yams as cash crops. These are planted in a three-year rotational system, alternating with cassava and a year of diverse crops including maize, peanuts, cotton, and beans.

The political and social systems vary greatly in different regions, and allegiance is uniformly paid to the large urban center in the area, rather than to a singular centralized authority.

The Yoruba claim that they have 401 deities; in truth, there are more than these. The complexity of their cosmology has led Western scholars to compare them to the ancient Greeks and their impressive pantheon. Yoruba deities are known as Orisha, and the high god is Olorun. There are no organized priesthoods or shrines in honor of Olorun, but his spirit is invoked to ask for blessings and to confer thanks.

Credits: Christopher D. Roy, Professor of the History of Art the University of Iowa; also see credit page.

ZULU

The Zulu tribe live in Natal Province in South Africa, with a population of 3 million people. Their spoken language is Kwazulu (Nguni). The AmaZulu believe that they are the direct descendants of the patriarch Zulu, who was born to a Nguni chief in the Congo Basin area. In the sixteenth century, the Zulu migrated southward to their present location, incorporating many of the customs of the San, including the well-known linguistic clicking sounds of the region. During the reign of King Shaka (1816-1828), the Zulu became the mightiest military force in southern Africa, increasing their land holdings from 100 square miles to 11,500. Shaka was followed by Dingaan, who tentatively entered into treaties with English colonizers. Mpande was the next king. He gave the British extensive control over his peoples. By the time he died in 1872, the Zulu had had enough of the French invasion. Rural Zulu raise cattle and farm corn and vegetables for subsistence purposes. The men and herd boys are primary responsible for the cows, which are grazed in the open country, while the women do most, if not all, of the planting and harvesting.

As is evident by the history of the Zulu, the leader, or chief, is invested with power based on his genealogy. He plays an important part in the internal governing of the Zulu homeland and also acts as a voice for his people on an international level. Although the Zulu are officially ruled by the government of South Africa, they often act as a dissenting voice on the national scene.

Zulu religion includes belief in a creator god (Nkulunkulu), who is above interacting in day-to-day human affairs. It is possible to appeal to the spirit world only by invoking the ancestors (AmaDlozi) through divination processes. As such, the diviner, who is almost always a woman, plays an important part in the daily lives of the Zulu.

Credits: Christopher D. Roy; also see credit page, Professor of the History of Art, the University of Iowa.

All these tribes coexisted peacefully and organized themselves correctly into real governments, endowed with all administrative and political processes, thanks to their own intelligence. The centralized monarchy of the Mossi-Dagombas, to the extremely elaborate organization, that had all features of a feudal state, to which only misses the bureaucracy of the one that copied the writings. The old theocracy of the Fouta Djallon had a real system of alternation in spite of the rivalry between two royal families, the Soriyas and the Alphayas. Without forgetting the theocratic state of Sekou Amadou, which imposed itself on the whole central delta of Niger, where it established a theocratic state having its capital, Hamdallahi.

The regime of Dina of the Macina seducing spatial organization and socio-cultural is the implementation of a religious inspiration utopia. Although austere, this order settled with measure and rationalities the questions of the daily life of West African in the nineteenth century puts in light the power of invention and initiative of the controlling elites of the time. Every entity has his specificity and his own genius. Model of elective monarchy doesn't exist truly, of theocracy or power lineage, adopted everywhere. Although the founding principles of these states can be the same .

It is this faculty of invention that has been lost since the colonization by the African political elites.

It's necessary to say that the traditional African society articulates on a certain number of beliefs whose foundations is in the cult of the ancestors, made of father and son according to a mostly patriarchal succession. Here the person who embodies the symbol of the society, as much political as religious, is the traditional chief who is at the same time a political and religious chief of the village. He is the big sacrifice maker even if he makes it by interposed peoples. The life of the traditional man is very marked by this cult of the ancestors, of which one thinks that they are in the "village of the blessed." So it is necessary to do all in order to be on good terms with the ancestors in order to be sure not to incur a possible punishment or malediction that could fall on us for a disobedience.

To the consideration of everything that has been said concerning traditional Africa, strength is to recognize that states and territories existed way before the modern age, endowed with all necessary institutions to manage the traditional society. These institutions include notably, the law of justice arbitration, the management of conflicts as well as the security and the army, to mention those only. To take only the sixteenth century, whose events marked again the collective memory of the populations, West Africa in particular saw fit to emerge or to coexist, here and there, of the social and political system of all kinds. The contest of history and anthropology is indispensable to seize the hidden sense of the dynamics of the traditional African societies.

Point of meeting of the peoples and the civilizations as heterogeneous as the Zulu, the Swahili, and the Bantu in the east and the Mandingos, the Malinke, and the Bambara in the west. Thank God the genius of the societies had good length of advance on the one of the politicians. Because of her regional variants and her innumerable ethnic groups and expressions, Africa exists altogether. And if she could survive the risks of history, but also the meanness, to the excessiveness and to the intolerance of her own sons, it's well because she takes advantage of a parking collective memory of a centennial trans-ethnic heritage. A motor calls another: who says memory says history, that is to say attitude in and towards the time. However, the African history would not know how to back out of the laws that govern the formation and evolution of the people if here, as elsewhere, she played fratricidal struggles to the will of the game of the contradictions and the interests of its context. How to wonder from the moment that he forged himself of this indispensable feeling of community of destiny that is the peoples, what was Arian the mythological thread?

With rare exception the oral character is near, the common denominator of the African cultural foundation. In African society, speech is well more than a prosaic tool of communication or presentation. How does the man have to proceed to express his poor person's conditions?

In appropriating itself to the manner of Prometheus stealing fire, with the difference that there, it will be about a sinuous course <initiatrix?> where the ruse supplants the challenge and where humility takes the step on bragging. Why risk the wrath of God?

Some men impose themselves for officer at the time of the ritual practice metaphysics to say it. These men, these will be the Griots, collectors of the Princes, confidants and advisers of the kings, historic mementos, living encyclopedias, poets, sociologists and moralists, they are in Africa what the Rabelaisians, the Dante, the servants, the Died rots and other the Brier are in Europe .

It's undoubtedly in the West African traditional societies that art of the Griot reaches its state of grace. Inherited from father and son, here he has value of system. Come out of the night of the times, he knew how to get married with happiness the subtleties to say it to an elegant and refined music. Who doesn't know the prestigious lineage of the 'Diéli' that Griot are ?

Almost everywhere in Africa, speech transports the same fund of proverbs, riddles, and tales while bewildering and ridiculing the ethnic or regional borders and the linguistic gates: Zulu, Swahili, Bantu or Mandingo, Wolof or Bambara. Rivalries and complicities. Specificities and mixture. Diversity and unit. Then all on the bottom of heathenism and oral tradition.

So that's your sauce, it doesn't miss anymore to this delicious mixture that the foreign ingredient without which the civilizations would be so flavorless. Here, this ingredient has two faces: the Judeo-Christian influence transported, of course, by the white Fathers and whose print especially carried on the inshore and forest peoples of the Continent, the Arab-Islamic influence brought by the Sudan-Swahelian peoples whose origins go back up the valley of the Nile. The eruption of these two currents mark a double rupture in the West African traditional society: the intrusion of the writing and the propagation of monotheism. Their impact will be decisive, shattering mentalities and closing that it's necessary to call a real cultural revolution of the ancestral traditional oral poetry, comes to pair itself a poetry written under the triple bucolic, mystical, and sentimental inspiration, today again in vogue in some African villages. This literary current lets to the posterity of the works worthy of the best flourishing, to the low of which, of the authors who could pretend comfortably to the universality without the weight of prejudices that choke our beautiful world, affixed their signature: Senghor, Camara Laye, Hampaté Bâ, and so on.

In West Africa, the Christian religion had a less happy fate. But she made the bed of the colonization of which the technological and cultural contributions came from, but also the trauma that was exercised on the African society, and the deep modifications made upon it, and, who knows? This could be a legacy that proves to be more lasting than that of Islam. Who ignored it?

Today, officially at least, almost all the West African countries are French-speaking, not Arab-speaking; they are secular states, not Muslim, in spite of the crushing majority of the disciples of Mohammed.

However, now we can rightly hope that West Africa's Pandora's box of slave trading and colonization will finally stop bring about so many misfortunes for them.

While continuing to pray for the deaths of these two afflicting periods, the Africans will know how to find the necessary springs to dress the injuries and to exercise the old demons.